D0989474

Success and Failure in Psychoanalysis and Psychotherapy

Success and Failure in Psychoanalysis and Psychotherapy

EDITED BY
Benjamin B. Wolman, Ph. D.

THE MACMILLAN COMPANY
New York, New York
COLLIER-MACMILLAN LIMITED   London

Acknowledgments

The origins of this volume go back to a panel discussion on "Success and failure in psychoanalytic therapy" held at the Sixth Annual Scientific Conference on Psychoanalytic Psychotherapy held in New York, on February 25, 1968 under the auspices of the Council of Psychoanalytic Psychotherapists. The panelists were Drs. Arnold Bernstein, Edward J. Hornick, Aaron Stein, Earl G. Witenberg and Benjamin B. Wolman (Chairman).

In preparation of this volume, I consulted my co-authors and also Drs. Kurt Adler, Jacob A. Arlow, Gustav Bychowski, Anna Freud, George Goldman, Heinz Hartmann, Mark Kanzer, Harold Kelman, Samuel Ritvo, and Victor H. Rosen.

The second chapter was re-translated from German and edited by Dr. Kurt Adler.

To all of them I convey my profound gratitude.

BENJAMIN B. WOLMAN

Preface

PSYCHOANALYSTS and psychotherapists often look down on the world from the height of their armchairs, seeing humanity stretched out on the couch. This time, however, we are going to take a look at ourselves, and try to analyze our own shortcomings and to discuss the difficulties we face in performing our professional duties.

One of the most important research problems in psychoanalytic or any other psychotherapeutic procedure is to determine whether one is successful and, if so, to what extent. The aim of treatment of mental disorders is success; that is why patients and hospitals pay fees and society supports therapeutic institutions, clinics and institutes. We are paid for being useful and helping people who need our help.

Are we helping people or are we falling short of our goal? Are we capable of performing the way we would like to? I must confess that the more one reads the results of research in the field, the more uncertain one is as to whether this research produces sufficiently clear and succinctly convincing evaluation of our work. Over the long years of clinical practice my own impression has been that the psychotherapeutic process, including psychoanalysis, is basically a *field process*. Whenever anyone asks the question, "Is schizophrenia, manic depressive disorder or any other mental ill curable, and, if so, to what degree?", or if someone asks, "What is the prognosis for this or another disturbance?", my own impression has been that the answer should be that it all depends on *who* is the patient, *who* his therapist is and *how* they interact.

Every psychotherapeutic process is a *process of interaction* in which two parties participate. The therapist and the patient are two interlocking parts of this psychodynamic field. Thus, research in psychotherapy and psychoanalysis must be performed on *field-theoretical* lines, not necessarily those of Kurt Lewin or any of the particular field-theories, but in a literary sense; the therapist and the patient are the poles of the field; they are dynamically interlocked, and the behavior of one of them affects the behavior of the other. The result of this interactional process does not depend merely on their particular personalities but also on how these two personalities influence one another. The outcome of this process depends on *who* influences *whom,* and how, and to what extent, and how successfully interaction took place. Finally the outcome is what counts.

Obviously, therapists are more successful with some patients than with others. Transference and countertransference are the key elements in the therapeutic process, and that is why the present volume starts with Freud's classic "Observations on Transference Love." The patient reacts to the analyst on the basis of childhood experience; he unconsciously transfers onto the analyst the feelings he has had in regard to his parents or parental substitutes. The therapist, whether he is an analyst or not, cannot help being influenced by his own past experiences and, to some extent, relates to his patient on the basis of emotional memories.

Yet, transference and countertransference are only a part of what is going on in consultation rooms. Besides being a convenient target for transference, the therapist or the psychoanalyst is a real human being; so is his patient. Their interaction includes several irrational elements derived from the past, but the interactional therapeutic process takes place here and now, and it is a real interaction between two individuals. This interaction transcends transference and countertransference.

Innumerable interactional patterns can take place between the two individuals. Taking into consideration all the possible personality variations of therapists and of patients, one may arrive at an astronomic calculus of possible interactional patterns.

Even the best method of treatment cannot produce satisfactory results if improperly applied. The tool that one uses in treatment of mental disorders is oneself: the psychoanalyst or the psychotherapist, his skills, intelligence, devotion, his total personality, are the most important healing factor. Success in treatment depends no less on the therapist's personality than on the method he uses. What one *is* may carry more weight than what one does.

My distinguished co-authors in this volume discuss several aspects of success and failure in psychoanalysis and psychotherapy. My own essay deals mainly with my shortcomings.

Benjamin B. Wolman

Contents

Acknowledgments   v
Preface   vii

PART ONE
Foundations

   I. Observations on Transference-Love   3
      SIGMUND FREUD (1915)

  II. The Concept of Resistance During Treat-
      ment   21
      ALFRED ADLER (1916)

PART TWO
Theoretical Explanations

   I. Causes of Failure in Psychoanalytic Psy-
      chotherapy   37
      AARON STEIN, M.D.

  II. Psychoanalysis and Its Relationship to
      Socioeconomic and Sociopolitical Change   53
      STANLEY LESSE, M.D., MED. SC.D.

 III. Ferment in Psychoanalysis and Psycho-
      analytic Psychotherapy   71
      HANS H. STRUPP, PH.D.

PART THREE
Clinical Experiences

   I. Some Problems in Psychoanalytic Tech-
      nique   107
      LEON J. SAUL, M.D.

CONTENTS

II. Remarks on Success and Failure in Psychoanalysis and Psychotherapy   131
   EDWARD GLOVER, M.D., LL.D., F.B.P.S.

III. Somato-psychic Interaction as Seen in Treatment Failures in a Mental Hospital   153
   HENRY BRILL, M.D.

IV. The Fear of Compassion   160
   ARNOLD BERNSTEIN, PH.D.

V. How Not to Succeed in Psychotherapy   177
   EARL G. WITENBERG, M.D.

VI. My Failures: Some of Them and How They Grew   193
   EDWARD J. HORNICK, M.D.

VII. Some Unsolved Problems of Psychoanalytic Psychotherapy   202
   LAWRENCE S. KUBIE, M.D.

VIII. The Working-through Phase—Failure to Focus   222
   BERNARD F. RIESS, PH.D

IX. The Human Factor in Psychoanalysis and Psychotherapy   232
   BENJAMIN B. WOLMAN, PH.D.

Contributors   253
Index of Names   257
Index of Subjects   260

PART ONE

Foundations

Observations on Transference-Love[1]

SIGMUND FREUD (1915)

EVERY beginner in psychoanalysis probably feels alarmed at first at the difficulties in store for him when he comes to interpret the patient's associations and deal with the reproduction of repressed material. When the time comes, however, he soon learns to look upon these difficulties as insignificant and instead becomes convinced that the only serious difficulties are encountered in handling the transference.

Among the situations to which the transference gives rise, one is very sharply outlined, and I will select this, partly because it occurs so often and is so important in reality and partly because of its theoretical interest. The case I mean is that in which a woman or girl patient shows by unmistakable allusions or openly avows that she has fallen in love, like any other mortal woman, with the physician who is analyzing her. This situation has its distressing and its comical aspects as well as its serious ones; it is so complicated, and conditioned by so many factors, so unavoidable and so difficult to dissolve, that discussion of it has long been a pressing need of analytic technique. But since those who mock at the failings of others are not always them-

[1] First published as Further Recommendations in the Technique of Psycho-analysis, in *Zeitschrift*, Bd. III., 1915. Reprinted in *Sammlung* Vierte Folge. Translated by Joan Riviere.

selves free from them, we have hardly been inclined to rush in to the fulfillment of this task. The obligation of professional discretion, which cannot be disregarded in life but which is useless in our science, makes itself felt here again and again. Insofar as psychoanalytical publications are a part of life, we have here an insoluble conflict. I have recently disregarded this matter of discretion for once [2] and shown how this same transference situation at first retarded the development of psychoanalytic therapy for ten years.

To a cultivated layman—and in their relation to psychoanalysis the attitude of such men is the best we encounter—matters concerned with love cannot be measured by the same standards as other things: it is as though they were written on a page by themselves which would not take any other script. If a patient falls in love with her doctor, such a man will think only two outcomes are possible—one comparatively rare, in which all the circumstances allow of a permanent legal union between them, and the other, much commoner, in which physician and patient part and abandon the work begun which should have led her to recovery, as though it had been prevented by some elemental phenomenon. There is certainly a third conceivable way out, which even appears compatible with continuing the treatment, and that is a love relationship between them of an illicit character, not intended to last permanently; but both conventional morality

[2] On the History of the Psycho-Analytic Movement, Collected Papers, Vol. 1, 1914.

and professional dignity surely make this impossible. In any event our layman would beg the analyst to reassure him as unambiguously as possible that this third alternative is out of the question.

It is clear that the analyst's point of view must be different from this.

Let us take the case of the second possible alternative. After the patient has fallen in love with the physician, they part; the treatment is given up. But very soon the patient's condition necessitates her making another attempt at cure with another physician; the next thing that happens is that she feels she has fallen in love with the second physician, and just the same again when she had broken off and begun again with a third, and so on. This phenomenon, which occurs with such regularity and is one of the foundations of psychoanalytical theory, may be regarded from two points of view, that of the physician analyzing and that of the patient in need of analysis.

To the physician it represents an invaluable explanation and a useful warning against any tendency to countertransference which may be lurking in his own mind. He must recognize that the patient's falling in love is induced by the analytic situation and is not to be ascribed to the charms of his person, that he has no reason whatever, therefore, to be proud of such a "conquest," as it would be called ouside analysis. And it is always well to be reminded of this. For the patient, however, there are two alternatives: either she must abandon her analytic treatment or she must make up her mind to being in love with physicians as to an inevitable destiny.[3]

I have no doubt that the patient's relatives and friends would decide as emphatically in favor of the first of the two alternatives as the analyst would for the second. In my opinion, however, this is a case in which the decision cannot be left to the tender—or rather, the jealous, egoistic—mercies of the relatives and friends. The patient's welfare alone should decide. The love of her relatives cannot cure her neurosis. It is not necessary for the psychoanalyst to force himself upon anyone, but he may take the stand that for certain purposes he is indispensable. Anyone who takes Tolstoy's attitude to this problem can remain in undisputed possession of his wife or daughter but must try to put up with her retaining her neurosis and with the disturbance it involves in her capacity for love. After all, it is the same situation as that of a gynecological treatment. Incidentally, the jealous father or husband makes a great mistake if he thinks the patient will escape falling in love with the physician if he hands her over to some other kind of treatment than that of analysis in order to get rid of her neurosis. On the contrary, the difference will be that her falling in love in a way which is bound to remain unexpressed and unanalyzed can never render that aid to her recovery which analysis would have extracted from it.

It has come to my knowledge that certain physicians

[3] We know that the transference can express itself by other less tender feelings, but I do not propose to go into that side of the matter here.

who practice analysis frequently prepare their patients for the advent of a love-transference or even instruct them to "go ahead and fall in love with the analyst so that the treatment may make progress." I can hardly imagine a more nonsensical proceeding. It robs the phenomenon itself of the element of spontaneity which is so convincing and it lays up obstacles ahead which are extremely difficult to overcome.

At first glance it certainly does not appear that any benefit to the treatment could result from the patient's falling in love in the transference. No matter how amenable she has been up till then, she now suddenly loses all understanding of and interest in the treatment, and will not hear or speak of anything but her love, the return of which she demands; she has either given up her symptoms or else she ignores them; she even declares herself well. A complete transformation ensues in the scene; it is as though some make-believe had been interrupted by a real emergency, just as when the cry of fire is raised in a theater. Any physician experiencing this for the first time will find it difficult to keep a grasp of the analytic situation and not to succumb to the illusion that the treatment is really at an end.

On reflection one realizes the true state of things. One remembers above all the suspicion that everything impeding the progress of the treatment may be an expression of resistance. It certainly plays a great part in the outbreak of passionate demands for love. One has long noticed in the patient the signs of an affectionate transference to the physician and could with certainty ascribe to this attitude her docility, her acceptance of the analytic explanations, her remarkable apprehension, and the high degree of intelligence which she displayed during this period. This is now all swept away; she has become completely lacking in understanding and seems to be swallowed up in her love; and this change always comes over her just as one brings her to the point of confessing or remembering one of the particularly painful or heavily repressed vicissitudes in her life history. She had been in love, that is to say, for a long time; but now the resistance is beginning to make use of it in order to hinder the progress of the treatment, to distract her interest from the work, and to put the analyst into a painful and embarrassing position.

If one looks into the situation more closely one can recognize that more complicated motives are also at work, of which some are connected with the falling in love and others are particular expressions of resistance. To the first belong the patient's efforts to reassure herself of her irresistibility, to destroy the physician's authority by bringing him down to the level of a lover, and to gain all the other advantages which she foresees as incidental to gratification of her love. With regard to the resistance, one may presume that at times it uses the declarations of love as a test for the strait-laced analyst, so that compliance on his part would call down on him a reprimand. But above all one obtains the impression that the resistance acts as an *agent provocateur,* intensifying the love of the patient and exaggerating her readiness for the sexual surrender, in

8

order thereby to vindicate the action of her repression more emphatically by pointing to the dangers of such licentiousness. All this by-play, which in less complicated cases may not be present at all, has, as we know, been regarded by A. Adler as the essential element in the whole process.

But how is the analyst to behave in this situation if he is not to come to grief and yet believes that the treatment should be continued through this love-transference and in spite of it?

It would be very simple for me now, on the score of conventional morality, to insist emphatically that the analyst must never in any circumstances accept or return the tender passion proffered him—that instead he must watch for his chance to urge the infatuated woman to take the moral path and see the necessity of renunciation, and induce her to overcome the animal side of her nature and subdue her passion, so as to continue the analytic work.

I shall not fullfil these expectations, however—neither the first nor the second. Not the first, because I am writing not for patients but for physicians who have serious difficulties to contend with, and also because of this instance I can go behind moral prescriptions to the source of them, namely, to utility. I am on this occasion in the happy position of being able to put the requirements of analytic technique in the place of a moral decree without any alteration in the results.

Even more emphatically, however, do I decline to fulfill the second of the expectations suggested above. To urge the patient to suppress, to renounce, and to sublimate the promptings of her instincts as soon as she has confessed her love-transference would be not an analytic way of dealing with them but a senseless way. It would be the same thing as to conjure up a spirit from the underworld by means of a crafty spell and then to dispatch him back again without a question. One would have brought the repressed impulses out into consciousness only in terror to send them back into repression once more. Nor should one deceive oneself about the success of any such proceeding. When leveled at the passions lofty language achieves very little, as we all know. The patient will feel only the humiliation, and will not fail to revenge herself for it.

Just as little can I advocate a middle course which would recommend itself to some as especially ingenious; this would consist in averring one's response to the patient's feelings of affection but in refraining from all the physical accompaniments of these tender feelings, until one could guide the situation along calmer channels and raise it onto a higher level. Against this expedient I have to object that the psychoanalytic treatment is founded on truthfulness. A great part of its educative effect and its ethical value lies in this very fact. It is dangerous to depart from this sure foundation. When a man's life has become bound up with the analytic technique he finds himself at a loss altogether for the lies and the guile which are otherwise so indispensable to a physician, and if for once with the best intentions he attempts to use them he is likely to betray himself. Since we demand strict truthfulness from our patients we jeopardize our whole authority if we let ourselves be caught by them in a departure from the truth. And besides, this experimental adoption of tender feeling for the patient is by no means without danger. One cannot keep such complete control of oneself as not one day suddenly to go further than was intended. In my opinion, therefore, it is not permissible to disavow the indifference one has developed by keeping the countertransference in check.

I have already let it be seen that the analytic technique requires the physician to deny the patient who is longing for love the satisfaction she craves. The treatment must be carried through in a state of abstinence; I do not mean merely corporal abstinence, nor yet deprivation of everything desired, for this could perhaps not be tolerated by any sick person. But I would state as a fundamental principle that the patient's desire and longing are to be allowed to remain, to serve as driving forces for the work and for the changes to be wrought, and that one must beware of granting this source of strength some discharge by surrogates. Indeed, one could not offer the patient anything but surrogates, for until the repressions are lifted her condition makes her incapable of true satisfaction.

Let us admit that this principle—of carrying through the analytic treatment in a state of renunciation—extends far beyond the case we are discussing, and that it needs close consideration in order to define the limits of its possible application. But we will refrain from going into this question now and will keep as closely as possible to the situation we started from. What would happen if the physician were to behave differently, and avail himself of a freedom perhaps available to them both to return the love of the patient and to appease her longing for tenderness from him?

If he had been guided in his decision by the argument that compliance on his part would strengthen his power over the patient so that he could influence her to perform the tasks required by the treatment, that is, could achieve a permanent cure of her neurosis by this means, experience would teach him that he had miscalculated. The patient would achieve her aim, but he would never achieve his. There is an amusing story about a pastor and an insurance agent which describes what would happen. An ungodly insurance agent lay at the point of death and his relatives fetched the holy man to convert him before he died. The interview lasted so long that those outside began to have some hope. At last the door of the sick chamber opened. The free-thinker had not been converted—but the pastor went away insured.

If her advances were returned it would be a great triumph for the patient, but a complete overthrow for the cure. She would have succeeded in what all patients struggle for, expressing in action, reproducing in real life, what she ought only to remember, to reproduce as the content of her mind, and to retain within the mental sphere.[4] In the further course of the love-relationship all the inhibitions and pathological reactions of her love-development would come out, yet

[4] Cf. *op. cit.* Vol. 2, pp. 321 and 369 *et seq.*

there would be no possibility of correcting them, and the painful episode would end in remorse and a strengthening of her tendency to repression. The love-relationship actually destroys the influence of the analytic treatment on the patient; a combination of the two would be an inconceivable thing.

It is therefore just as disastrous for the analysis if the patient's craving for love prevails as if it is suppressed. The way the analyst must take is neither of these; it is one for which there is no prototype in real life. He must guard against ignoring the transference-love, scaring it away or making the patient disgusted with it; and just as resolutely must he withhold any response to it. He must face the transference-love boldly but treat it like something unreal, as a condition which must be gone through during the treatment and traced back to its unconscious origins, so that it shall assist in bringing to light all that is most hidden in the development of the patient's erotic life and help her to learn to control it. The more plainly the analyst lets it be seen that he is proof against every temptation, the sooner will the advantage from the situation accrue to the analysis. The patient, whose sexual repressions are of course not yet removed but merely pushed into the background, will then feel safe enough to allow all her conditions for loving, all the fantasies of her sexual desires, all the individual details of her way of being in love to come to light, and then will herself open up the way back from them to the infantile roots of her love.

With one type of woman, to be sure, this attempt to

13

preserve the love-transference for the purposes of analytic work without gratifying it will not succeed. These are women of an elemental passionateness; they tolerate no surrogates; they are children of nature who refuse to accept the spiritual instead of the material; to use the poet's words, they are amenable only to the "logic of gruel and the argument of dumplings." With such people one has the choice either to return their love or else to bring down upon oneself the full force of the mortified woman's fury. In neither event can one safeguard the interests of the treatment. One must acknowledge failure and withdraw; and may at leisure study the problem how the capacity for neurosis can be combined with such an intractable craving for love.

Many analysts must have discovered the way in which other women, less violent in their love, can be brought round gradually to the analytic point of view. Above all, the unmistakable element of resistance in their "love" must be insisted upon. Genuine love would make the patient docile and intensify her readiness to solve the problems of her case, simply because the man she loved expected it. A woman who was really in love would gladly choose the road to completion of the cure in order to give herself value in the physician's eyes and to prepare herself for real life, where her feelings of love could find their proper outlet. Instead of this she is showing a stubborn and rebellious spirit, has thrown up all interest in her treatment and clearly, too, all respect for the physician's well-founded judgment. She is bringing out a resistance, therefore, under the guise of being in love; and in addition to this, she has no compunction about trying to lead him into a cleft stick. For if he refuses her love, as duty and his understanding compel him to do, she can take the attitude that she has been humiliated and, out of revenge and resentment, make herself inaccessible to cure by him, just as she is now doing ostensibly out of love.

One advances a second argument against the genuineness of this love by the fact that it shows not a single new feature connecting it with the present situation but is entirely composed of repetitions and "rechauffés" of earlier reactions, including childish ones. One then sets about proving this by detailed analysis of the patient's behavior in love.

When the necessary amount of patience is added to these arguments it is usually possible to overcome the difficult situation and to continue the work, the patient having either moderated her love or transformed it; the aim of the work then becomes the discovery of the infantile object-choice and of the fantasies woven round it. I will now, however, examine these arguments critically and put the question whether they really represent the truth or whether by employing them we are not in our desperation resorting to prevarication and misrepresentation. In other words: Can the love which is manifested in analytic treatment not truly be called real?

I think that we have told the patient the truth, but not the whole truth without regard for consequences. Of our two arguments the first is the stronger. The part taken by resistance in the transference-love is unquestionable and very considerable. But this love was not created by the resistance. The second argument is far weaker; it is true that the love consists of new editions of old traces and that it repeats infantile reactions. But this is the essential character of every love. There is no love that does not reproduce infantile prototypes. The infantile conditioning factor in it is just what gives it its compulsive character which verges on the pathological. The transference-love has perhaps a degree less of freedom than the love which appears in ordinary life and is called normal; it displays its dependence on the infantile pattern more clearly, is less adaptable and capable of modification, but that is all and that is nothing essential.

By what other signs can the genuineness of a love be recognized? By its power to achieve results, its capacity to accomplish its aim? In this respect the transference-love seems to give place to none; one has the impression that one could achieve anything by its means.

Let us resume, therefore: One has no right to dispute the "genuine" nature of the love which makes its appearance in the course of analytic treatment. However lacking in normality it may seem to be, this quality is sufficiently explained when we remember that the condition of being in love in ordinary life outside analysis is also more like abnormal than normal mental phenomena. The transference-love is characterized, nevertheless, by certain features which ensure it a special position. In the first place, it is provoked by the analytic situation; secondly, it is greatly intensified by the resistance which dominates this situation; and thirdly, it is to a high degree lacking in regard for reality, is less sensible, less concerned about consequences, more blind in its estimation of the person loved than we are willing to admit of normal love. We should not forget, however, that it is precisely these departures from the norm that make up the essential element in the condition of being in love.

The first of these three characteristics of the transference-love is what determines the physician's course of action. He has evoked this love by undertaking analytic treatment in order to cure the neurosis; for him it is an unavoidable consequence of the medical situation, as inevitable as the exposure of a patient's body, of being told some life-and-death secret. It is therefore plain to him that he is not to derive any personal advantage from it. The patient's willingness makes no difference whatever; it merely throws the whole responsibility on him. Indeed, as he must know, the patient had from the beginning entertained hopes of this way of being cured. After all the difficulties are overcome she will often confess to a fantasy, an expectation, that she had had as she began the treatment—"if she behaved well, she would be rewarded in the end by the doctor's love for her."

For the physician there are ethical motives which combine with the technical reasons to hinder him from according the patient his love. The aim that he has to keep in view is that this woman, whose capacity for love is disabled by infantile fixations, should attain complete access to this function, which is so inestimably important for her in life, not that she should fritter it away in the treatment but preserve it for real life, if it be that after her cure life makes that demand on her. He must not let the scene of the race between the dogs be enacted, in which the prize was a chaplet [garland, wreath] of sausages and which a funny fellow spoiled by throwing one sausage onto the course; the dogs fell upon it and forgot about the race and the chaplet in the distance luring them on to win. I do not mean to say that it is always easy for the physician to keep within the bounds prescribed by technique and ethics. Younger men especially, who are not yet bound by a permanent tie, may find it a hard task. The love between the sexes is undoubtedly one of the first things in life, and the combination of mental and bodily satisfaction attained in the enjoyment of love is literally one of life's culminations. Apart from a few perverse fanatics, all the world knows this and conducts life accordingly; only science is too refined to confess it. Again, when a woman sues for love, to reject and refuse is a painful part for a man to play; and in spite of neurosis and resistance there is an incomparable fascination about a noble woman who confesses her passion. It is not the grossly sensual desires of the patient that constitute the temptation. These are more likely to repel and to demand the exercise of toleration in order to regard them as a natural phenomenon. It is perhaps the finer impulses, those "inhibited in their aim," which lead a man into the danger of forgetting the rules of technique and the physician's task for the sake of a wonderful experience.

And yet the analyst is absolutely debarred from giving way. However highly he may prize love, he must prize even more highly the opportunity to help his patient over a decisive moment in her life. She has to learn from him to overcome the pleasure-principle, to give up a gratification which lies to hand but is not sanctioned by the world she lives in, in favor of a distant and perhaps altogether doubtful one which is, however socially and psychologically unimpeachable. To achieve this mastery of herself she must be taken through the primordial era of her mental development and in this way reach that greater freedom within the mind which distinguishes conscious mental activity—in the systematic sense—from unconscious.

The analytic psychotherapist thus has a threefold battle to wage: in his own mind against the forces which would draw him down below the level of analysis; outside analysis against the opponents who dispute the importance he attaches to the sexual instinctual forces and hinder him from making use of them in his scientific method; and in the analysis against his patients, who at first behave like his critics but later on disclose the overestimation of sexual life which has them in thrall, and who try to take him captive in the net of their socially ungovernable passions.

The lay public, of whose attitude to psychoanalysis I spoke at the outset, will certainly seize the opportunity given it by this discussion of the transference-love to direct the attention of the world to the dangers of this therapeutic method. The psychoanalyst knows that the forces he works with are of the most explosive kind and that he needs as much caution and conscientiousness as a chemist. But when has it ever been forbidden to a chemist, on account of its danger, to occupy himself with the explosives which, just because of their effectiveness, are so indispensable? It is remarkable that psychoanalysis has to win for itself afresh all the liberties which have long been accorded to other medical work. I certainly do not advocate that the harmless methods of treatment should be abandoned. For many cases they suffice, and when all is said, the *furor sanandi* is no more use to human society than any other kind of fanaticism. But it is grossly to undervalue both the origins and the practical significance of the psychoneuroses to suppose that these disorders are to be removed by pottering about with a few harmless remedies. No; in medical practice there will always be room for the *"ferrum"* and the *"ignis"* as well as for the *"medicina,"* and there a strictly regular, unmodified psychoanalysis, which is not afraid to handle the most dangerous forces in the mind and set them to work for the benefit of the patient, will be found indispensable.

The Concept of Resistance During Treatment

ALFRED ADLER (1916)

AMONG the symptoms of neuroses we find, in-
variably, a complex of manifestations which
are most common, most human, yet little understood.
We perceive these as obstinacy, stubbornness, contrar-
iness, hostility, and generally as a fighting attitude;
then again, as righteousness, dogmatism, and craving
for power. Here, too, belong the clinical concepts of
negativism, withdrawal, and autism (Bleuler). Attempts by the patient to defend such attitudes are
hardly ever absent; this is seen also in the psychoses.
Such rigidity is always indicative of a lack of ability to
cooperate, which is the only valid measure for comparison with the norm.

In this negativistic posture toward his fellow men
we can see the patient's total erroneous tendency to
isolation, his impotent and discouraged lust for power,
and his empty vanity. The disparaging attitude of the
patient, frequently camouflaged as meekness, obedi-
ence, love, or inferiority feelings, but always ineffectual and socially detrimental, is naturally also expressed toward the physician. The physician, however,
has the advantage of seeing also this aspect of the
patient's personality, then, to deprive the patient of

every opening for his attack, to interpret every pertinent expression, and to train the patient's ability to cooperate.[1]

A patient who had been under individual-psychological treatment for two months came to me one day and asked whether she could not come the next time at four o'clock instead of three. No matter how much patients, in such and similar cases, plead the necessity of their requests we are justified in assuming that the desired postponement is an indication of intensified aggression against the physician. We would be wrong and would be acting in direct opposition to the purpose of the treatment, which is to enable the patient to gain inner freedom, if we did not attempt on such occasions to investigate the reasons for the request.

The patient claimed that she would have to go to the dressmaker at three o'clock, a rather weak reason, which was only slightly strengthened by the fact that owing to the length of the treatment the number of free hours was somewhat restricted. As I was not free at the hour she asked for, I suggested, as a test, five or six. This the patient rejected with the remark that her mother would be free at five and expected her at a friend's house. Again we see an insufficient reason advanced, and are consequently justified in assuming that the patient is showing resistance to the treatment.

[1] "The above two paragraphs are missing in the English translation; I feel that they are important, a good introduction to the chapter, and telling of Adler's attitude. I, therefore translated these first two paragraphs myself. They were never translated before."—Kurt A. Adler, M.D.

Freud has repeatedly pointed out that analysis must start with these resistance phenomena which are, furthermore, frequently or always connected with transference. Since according to our view the psychic relations for these two phenomena are different, and are occasionally misunderstood, I shall attempt to discuss them on the basis of this case.

What we have first to consider in the analysis of the treatment is the particular point at which resistance asserted itself. In the case we are discussing, the patient had been talking for a few days about her relations to her brother. She told me that occasionally, when alone with him, she experienced an inexplicable feeling of disgust. She had, however, no feeling of aversion to him and gladly went with him to parties or the theater. But she was careful not to offer him her arm on the street lest strangers might mistake her for his mistress. She often conversed with him at home, and frequently permitted him to kiss her, a practice in which he liked to indulge. Kissing was one of her most passionate pleasures and at times she experienced a veritable kissing-mania. Of late she had been more reserved toward her brother because, owing to her acute sense of smell, she had noticed that his breath had a disgusting odor.

The patient's psychological relation to her brother is thus clear enough. She finds in herself certain emotions, and considers certain possibilities against which she immediately takes safeguarding steps. As the former stirrings take the form of female desires (to be kissed, to take the arm of a male companion), she answers them with the masculine protest, though veiled in an inconspicuous form.

What does she do to maintain her masculine attitude toward her brother? Unconsciously she introduces a false evaluation, develops such remarkable and fine perceptions and prophetic vision that she is occasionally quite right in her inference.[2]

The fear of being mistaken for her brother's mistress if she gives him her arm will be understood only by those who have had a similar attitude toward one of their siblings. She is quite right about the odor from her brother's mouth, although it is rather peculiar that no one else in the immediate circle of relations who are frequently kissed by him seems to have noticed it. Our patient has consequently made a re-evaluation unfavorable to her brother, indicating clearly what her object is. Some people would perhaps in this case only hear her "no." [3]

[2] A maniac may also be in the right. If I am to perform a task, and this is often to be done with patients mutatis mutandis, and discover a real typographical error, I am right when I point this out, even if I do it repeatedly. However, we are concerned with a task and not with the pointing out of a printer's error.

[3] False evaluations, whether under- or over-evaluations, are of the greatest importance in the psychical dynamics of normal life and of neurosis, and merit the most detailed study on the part of individual psychology. The "fox and the sour grapes" represents an instructive example. Instead of realizing his own inferiority, the fox depreciates the grapes, and thus retains his high spirits. He is intent on megalomania. This sort of psychical procedure primarily serves the maintenance, the fiction, of "free will," and with that, of personal worth. The same purpose is served by the over-evaluations of personal achievements and aims, caused by the individual's flight from the pessimistic feeling of his own inferiority. They are "ar-

If anyone doubts the likelihood of the existence of sexual feelings between brother and sister, instead of calling attention to the extensive data furnished by history and what can be obtained from criminal statistics and pedagogical experiences, I would merely insist that I do not regard them as possessing any great depth. It seems to me that it is very much a case of brother and sister playing "father and mother" in the nursery, where the girl, by reason of her neurotic masculine attitude, attempts to safeguard herself in order not to go too far. Her brother has long ceased to be her brother, but occupies the role of the future suitor. She lives with him in a world of fancy where she tries to show what she is capable of, and in what way she is planning to protect herself.[4] Besides, all incestuous stirrings

ranged" and arise out of an exaggerated safeguarding tendency directed against the feeling of "being below." That the exaggerated masculine attitude of male and female neurotics utilizes to the full this "arrangement" I have shown repeatedly. Also, the senses of the patient—hearing, smelling, vision, and skin, organ and pain sensations—all strained by the concentration on them, are put into the service of this safeguarding tendency, so that the patient becomes the judge and the culprit rolled into one. Compare Schiller's epigram: "You are right, Schlosser, we love what we possess and desire that which we do not own! Because only the rich soul loves, whereas the poor one lusts!" Once the patient actually understands his attitude, he corrects it by bringing his values into harmony with the facts of reality. His adaptation and cooperation begin with his feeling himself an equal.

[4] This anticipatory thinking, anticipatory perception with its accompanying safeguarding tendencies, is one of the main functions of the dream, and forms, among other things, the basis of what seems to be telepathic and prophetic happenings, but is also the essence of every form of prognosis. The poet Simonides was once, in a

point to a lack of ability to cooperate, and the patient, accordingly, often overcommitted to his family, will not extend himself beyond its limits.

Her recollections and the surviving emotional traces of past events tell her, however, what she is capable of. The total impression the patient receives is the following: "I am a girl, not strong enough to conquer my sexual desires; even in childhood I possessed little energy, my fancy playing with forbidden objects, and I was not even able to control myself with my brother! I will be calumniated and maltreated; I will be sick, bear children in pain, be conquered, be a slave! I must therefore, from the beginning and at all times, be on my guard, not succumb to my desires, not subject myself to a man, indeed, mistrust all men—by behaving, myself, like a man!" Her feminine sexual feelings become her enemy and this enemy she endows with unbelievable powers and wiles. Thus there arises in the emotional life of the neurotic a caricature of the sexual drive which it is really worth-while fighting. The male neurotic, likewise, fears those emotions he regards as feminine, such as tenderness, desire to subordinate himself to a woman, which make their appearance in his love-life, and which he consequently caricaturizes in order to fight them the more. From other, nonsexual relations, he obtains analogies: psychological traits,

dream, warned by one who was dead against embarking on a certain sea trip. He stayed at home and was afterwards informed that the particular boat had sunk. We may well assume that this famous poet, who had so "pointedly" argued against this journey, would probably have stayed at home even if he had not had this dream and this warning.

former weakness, indolence, listlessness, and early infantile errors.[5] All serve as evidence of the presence of nonmasculine, i.e., feminine, traits and are answered by the masculine protest. That real accidents are "arranged" or put into effect, that the defiant attitude enables female patients (this holds for girls who show defiance of their mother's warnings) to employ their own female sexual activity in the form of the masculine protest, and enables male neurotics to avoid the love relation by resorting to feminine softness and abulia (in the case of so-called "neurasthenia"), impotence and fear, all this I have discussed in other sections of this book. These "arranged" and frequently caricatured inner perceptions find a place in the woof and warp of the psyche and serve as warning signs that are to call forth powerfully the masculine protest and the protections against succumbing.

We have thus come to the conclusion that the patient hardly runs any danger today of committing incest, and that in her desire to safeguard herself she has gone further than was really necessary, but that by so acting she has served one of the main objects of her

[5] I had some patients who were always glad to point out (acc. to Fliess) the periodicity of their attacks, thus directing attention to their feminine "nature," but thereby betraying to me the fact that they had remained under the influence of a fundamental doubt—"am I masculine or feminine?" Theory, of course, assuages them: Everybody is part masculine and part feminine! When analyzed I always encounter some evidence that the periodicity of these attacks is being used as a means of resistance against the physician. But the patient is always implicated in arranging the periodicity of the attack. Recidivists and cyclothymics, however, attach themselves each time to a new difficulty.

masculine protest, namely, to shape her future independent of any man, and not in a feminine role.

The depreciation of the partner is a regular manifestation among neurotics. This fact may appear quite clearly, as in the example above, or it may be so completely disguised that some people, looking at their material, would find it impossible to conclude from it on the general validity of my statement. Frequently enough we do discover in neurotics masochistic and "feminine" traits and far-reaching tendencies toward subordination and suggestibility for hypnotism. The hysterical longing for the great, strong man before whom one can bend one's knees has always fascinated us! How many of the neurotic patients are full of admiration for their physician and chant hymns of praise to his honor! They act as though in love. But the obverse side turns up after a while,[6] for none can stand submission. They argue as follows: "What a weakling I am to be capable of such submission! I must safeguard myself with all means, in order not to succumb!" And like a person about to make a high jump they withdraw a few steps and duck, in order to jump, with increased power, over the other. One of my patients frequently said that she was amoral, and was at all times ready to enter into an affair. Unfortunately, men repulsed her aesthetically. Another patient who was being treated for impotence had been previously hypnotized for it by a charlatan. Upon leaving, this hypnotizer had told the patient that if he would put the fob

[6] Cf. my discusson of pseudomasochism in the "Psychic Treatment of Trigeminal Neuralgia."

of his watch around his head he would fall asleep. The patient was not cured of his impotence, but the experiment with sleep worked every time. He visited many physicians after this and whenever their medicine or mechanical treatment was ineffectual he asked to be hypnotized, which none were able to do. Thereupon at the end of the visit, he took out his fob and showed the physician how he put himself to sleep. The meaning of his behavior was: "You cannot even do what a charlatan did; you cannot even do what a fob can!" As soon as the patient, who always had been distrustful and interested in depreciating men and women, became aware of the secret of his psyche, the fob lost its power.

Whenever I traced this depreciatory attitude toward the masculine to its origin I always found it rooted in some infantile pathogenic situation in which the patient as a child already desired to get the better of his father, and either in actuality, or in his imagination, tried out all the fighting stances against his father, his brothers, and his teachers. But it seems also quite clear that the neurotic character of the disposed child, his exaggerated envy and ambition, greatly whips up his lust for power.

From this viewpoint it is easy to grasp the double role of the neurotically disposed child in his relation to women and also easy to test it by means of the data obtained. On the one hand, woman—like everything we cannot obtain immediately—is idealized in the most exaggerated manner and endowed with all the magic qualities of strength and power. Mythology, folktales, and folk beliefs frequently deal with a type of giantess, of female-demon—as in Heine's poem "The Lorelei" —where the man is represented as microscopically small or hopelessly lost. The neurotic frequently retains terrifying traces of his infantile attitude, conscious or unconscious fantasies, or protected memories (Freud) and reminiscences of women who towered above him or walked over him (cf. Ganghofer's biography and similar statements in Stendhal). All these scenes are to be understood not as trauma but as indicative of the life style. Later on, a feeling of timidity in the presence of women or the fear of remaining tied to them of not being able to get loose from them, is found expressed in one form or another in the psychical superstructure. Against this pressing psychic relation which threatens to subordinate him to a woman, the neurotic directs all his safeguarding tendencies, strengthens his masculine protest and his ideas of grandeur, and by means of these unconscious safeguarding tendencies humiliates and depreciates woman. Quite often, two types of female figures emerge in his fantasies and in his consciousness: Lorelei and (Wiswamitras) beloved; the ideal and the coarse-realistic figure; the mother (Mary) type and the prostitute (cf. O. Weininger). In other cases, either a composite form arises, like the real hetaira, or one of two types appears very definitely in the foreground (feminist and antifeminist).

When not more than six months old the child is known to reach out for all objects and is unwilling to give them up. Shortly after that, under the pressure of the striving for mastery and the social feeling, he takes hold of people who treat him well. Jealousy is the safeguarding tendency accompanying this desire for possession.[7] If the child is forced to make further anticipatory safeguards (uncertainty as to his sex role), then an early sexual maturity and timidity often arises. I have come to the conclusion that in the relation of the child to his parents, a subsequent neurotic trait is already operative which attempts a goal of god-likeness and at the same time tries to safeguard himself against defeat, by use of the hesitant attitude and a refusal to cooperate. The forms of infantile experiences as such possess no driving force; they are not causes but merely landmarks. They are, however, in the individual power-perspective recognized, employed, remembered, or forgotten. They have obtained recognition only because they portray striking manifestations of the dynamics of the neurotic, and, furthermore, because they can be utilized in the neurosis as reminders or types of expression within the framework of the masculine protest. "I am a weakling in regard to women! As a child I already subjected myself, in the form of love, to a

[7] In a hebephrenic I found this form of safeguarding extraordinarily strong. She showed an unconquerable tendency to tie to herself everything that belonged to her: husband, child, clothes, hats, her own toys, friends who visited her, as well as apartment and place where she had been longer. The example of a tyrannical mother and her own lust for power, which was symbolized by her daily walk, with enthusiasm, in a cemetery, gave the explanation. Understandably, her lust for power with the physician led to resistance, especially because his interpretations threatened her continued domination.

woman." Reading between the lines this means, "I am afraid of women." Immediately following this "demonic" influence of woman, her "puzzling nature," her "eternal inexplicability," her "compelling power," we find man either resorting to depreciation or flight. Psychic impotence, ejaculatio praecox, syphilophobia, and fear of love or marriage because of inability to cooperate then supervene. If the masculine protest manages to assert itself in the direction of sexual intercourse, the neurotic finds either the completely debased woman, the prostitute, the child, or the corpse [8] worthy of his love, or the strong woman whom he attempts to depreciate. Analysis subsequently discloses the real motive, the belief that he can control and rule either one more easily. Thus the masculine protest forces a man, afraid of facing reality, into the role of a Don Juan.[9]

I have never met a masculine neurotic who has not in some form or other laid particular stress on and tried to prove the inferiority of women, and probably, at the same time, of men. The fight against a rival in love arises out of the latter tendency [10] and is primarily envy. The female neurotic even more consistently depreciates both man and woman. Our patient, as she is dealing with a male physician, resorts, as on other

[8] That is, objects incapable of resistance, of deceit, or domination.

[9] Many women at the same time or closely following each other; never permanent. Only the sensation of a transitory victory not entailing any return on their part entices such people.

[10] Cf. also the corresponding behavior of the patient in the chapter on "Psychic Treatment of Trigeminal Neuralgia," *op. cit.*

occasions, to a depreciation of the newly appearing man. This she does all the more if she realizes that he is "superior" to her in knowledge. In the present case her "resistance" set in after I had explained to her important facts about the rebellious character of her neurosis. She countered with a new protest, "Because you were correct in so many things." But she wished to be in the right! If in her dream or in day fantasies she drew pictures in which she represented herself as frivolous or wicked and entertained thoughts of sexual relations with her brother or with me, this is to be understood as a neurotic exaggeration designed to safeguard her against just these things. This "love-transference" to the physician is consequently fictitious, to be interpreted as a caricature and not to be taken as "libido." It is in reality no (real) "transference" but simply an attitude and habit going back to childhood and representing the road to power. The further development was typical. The final struggle for the depreciation of the physician began. She knew everything better, and could do it better than the doctor. Hardly an hour would pass without her attempting by means of objections and reproaches of the most flagrant kind to undermine his medical prestige.

The means at the disposal of Individual Psychology suffice amply for eradicating the patient's mistrust against people. Patience, prevision, and predictions secure for the physician further progress. The progress consists in disclosing to the patient the specific pathogenic infantile situation in which his or her masculine protest is rooted. The friendly relation to the physician permits both patient and physician to get a complete insight into the neurotic activity, to realize the falsity of the emotional stirrings, the erroneous assumptions made by the neurotic disposition, and the neurotic's needless expenditure of energy. From the Individual-Psychologist the patient learns for the first time in his life to know himself, cooperation and the control of his overexcited drives. To accomplish this it is necessary to resolve the resistance against the physician. The physician connects with the patient through the vestiges of his social feeling that survive in the neurotic and psychically ill individual.

In a curious way our concepts about resistance parallel the statements of Pestalozzi's in *Lienhard und Gertrud* in regard to another failure of development: "People, who have been so long neglected find in every course of law and order to which one wants to lead them an unbearable yoke. You will find, if your purpose is to go deeper than just the surface, and if you don't want just to play a comedy with them, that they are all against you, that they will cheat you at every point and will try to hide everything from you. You will learn that the long and deeply brutalized man hates, in every relationship, the one who wants to pull him out of his condition, and treats him like an enemy."

PART TWO
Theoretical Explanations

Causes of Failure in Psychoanalytic Psychotherapy

AARON STEIN, M.D.

PSYCHOANALYTIC psychotherapy—or, more accurately, psychoanalytically oriented psychotherapy—is widely used as a form of psychotherapy. It is probably the most extensively used form of intensive psychotherapy and is generally considered to be, in well-trained hands and next to psychoanalysis, a very effective form of treatment.

In this paper an attempt will be made to discuss possible sources of failure in this form of psychotherapy. While the majority of patients—probably 60 to 80 percent—respond more or less favorably to psychoanalytic psychotherapy, a considerable number respond poorly or not at all. This is true even when the patients are carefully selected and the treatment is skillfully given.

DEFINITION, GOALS, AND LIMITATIONS

In order to understand why failures occur in this form of treatment, it is necessary to indicate the conditions that are set up and the goals that are sought in this form of psychotherapy. These have been discussed in detail elsewhere (Tarachow and Stein, 1967) and will be summarized here.

The various forms of psychotherapy may be usefully classified as follows: psychoanalysis, psychoanalytic psychotherapy, and supportive psychotherapy—in order of decreasing intensity. The difference between these would be related to the way in which the transference and resistance would be handled in each.

Psychoanalysis would be that form of psychotherapy in which conditions would be set up to focus the transference as freely as possible upon the analyst so that transference, and, especially, transference as a resistance, can be uncovered—i.e., made conscious and analyzed (interpreted)—to the fullest possible extent. In *psychoanalytic psychotherapy,* the transference would be permitted to a greater or lesser extent to remain uninterpreted as a resistance; the uncovering and analysis of other types of resistance would be attempted only partially and in accordance with the patient's needs. In *supportive psychotherapy,* the transference would remain largely uninterpreted and other resistances would also remain largely unexposed and uninterpreted and some defenses, according to the needs of the patient, may even be strengthened. The indications for these three types of treatment may be summarized as follows:

Psychoanalysis is the treatment of choice for patients with relatively intact personalities and ego strength, in whom unconscious conflicts have led to the development of neurotic symptoms and/or mild to moderately severe characterological disturbances and who can freely develop the necessary transference to the analyst. Freud designated such conditions as the "transference neuroses" in contrast to the "narcissistic neuroses," in which the libidinal cathexes were focused too rigidly on the self, making it difficult for the patient to develop the necessary type of transference.

Psychoanalytic psychotherapy would be indicated for patients whose underlying unconscious conflicts are more narcissistic in nature and whose ego strength and personality structure have undergone considerable deformation or weakening; the psychotherapy would be used to uncover some of the unconscious conflicts but without focusing an intense transference neurosis upon the therapist, so that the patient would not experience marked regressive change and would be subject to less intense frustration in the therapy. This type of treatment would therefore be used for patients with neurotic symptoms together with fairly severe characterological disturbances and/or borderline conditions with increased narcissistic tendencies and considerable impairment of reality testing.

Supportive psychotherapy would be most useful for patients whose ego strength and personality structure have been very considerably distorted and weakened and whose underlying unconscious conflicts tend toward the more primitive and narcissistic type. Patients who would fall into this group would be psychotics, particularly those in remission, borderline cases with severe characterological disturbances, and patients with severe narcissistic tendencies.

Returning now to psychoanalytic psychotherapy, the important point is the deliberate technical limitation set up in this form of treatment. This is the fact that the unconscious aspects of the transference as a resistance and the other types of resistance are only partially uncovered and only partially interpreted, or, putting it in the opposite way, certain parts of the transference and certain kinds of resistance remain uninterpreted. This technique is specifically chosen so as to provide support for the patient in the treatment and to help him in dealings with his conflicts and tensions and also in order to limit the extent of exploration of unconscious conflicts which could produce amounts of anxiety that might be difficult for the patient to handle. As many writers have pointed out (Gill, 1954; Rangell, 1954; Tarachow, 1963), this technical limitation distinguishes psychoanalytic psychotherapy from psychoanalysis and makes it a specifically useful form of treatment for the type of patient indicated above.

Because certain aspects of the transference remain uninterpreted in the formal treatment, the relationship to the therapist is seen by the patient as a real relationship and this provides a certain amount of gratification of the patient's object needs of the therapist. Tarachow (1963), Greenson (1965), and others have discussed at length and made the point that this gratification provides the support and energy for the patient to work in the treatment. Obviously, great care must be taken in such a form of treatment that the gratification of the transference may be accomplished carefully and that it should serve a useful purpose in strengthening the patient, supporting him and enabling him to work in the treatment without further regression or increasing anxieties.

Also, technically, this means that the therapist, for example, uses other methods, in contrast to the orthodox, or classical, form of analysis, of dealing with the patient, in addition to interpretation. In analysis his attitudes would be carefully maintained so as not to provide any gratification in the treatment situation, and his interventions would be carefully limited to interpretations of varying degrees and appropriate timing. In psychoanalytic psychotherapy he steps out of this role and actively discusses various things with the patient. He also actively provides support for the patient in various ways. For instance, he does this by prescribing medication, making himself available for telephone calls, and by offering a certain amount of advice, suggestion, or encouragement.

In doing this the danger is that if his attitude and technique are not the proper ones, he may gratify the transference beyond the limits of what the therapy requires and foster a regressive dependence on the therapist together with the continuance of unrealistic attitudes and expectations of the therapist.

This is further complicated because certain aspects of the treatment situation are real. The patient sees the therapist as a real person; notices certain reactions or attitudes of his, knows something about his life and activities to some degree, and gets something from the therapist in terms of greetings or goodbyes and various other interchanges. This is true in psychoanalysis as well as in psychoanalytic psychotherapy. The need of the patient is to obtain from the therapist some sort of object relationship which would provide the support and gratification he needs in dealing with the frustrations that come up in the treatment.

The need of the therapist is also one for object relationships. Very often one of the major difficulties is that the patient and the therapist unwittingly use each other to fulfill certain object needs and certain kinds of gratification.

Several writers (Gill, 1954; Stone, 1961) have stressed this and Tarachow (1963) discusses it in some detail:

The therapeutic test for the therapist as well as for the patient is his own struggle with his need for objects amidst a self-imposed therapeutic barrier, a barrier of denying himself object need. The problem of spontaneous and unplanned acts of the analyst arises from this consideration. The temptation to breach the barrier, to reach out to the patient for object gratification, assails the therapist at all times. If the patient pleads for help, the therapist wants to extend himself. If the patient is hostile, the therapist wants to fight. If the patient is unhappy, the therapist wants to console him. If the patient is in need, the therapist wants to give. The principal temptation for the therapist is to play the role of the good mother. For these reasons, it is necessary for the therapist to observe himself constantly for any alteration in his behavior towards the patient. When such alteration in behavior occurs, the therapist has joined in collusion with the patient in taking some aspect of the patient's behavior as real and has responded to it in some real but non-therapeutic way.

This does not mean that the therapist cannot, in this form of psychotherapy, indicate or express some feeling or attitude or gratify in some way the patient's need for help, providing that he maintains the therapeutic role. The therapeutic role for the therapist in this form of psychotherapy is one in which he is calm, sympathetic, interested, and helpful, but in a therapeutic way.

Contrary to what some other writers have advocated, it does not mean that the therapist plays roles or goes out of his way to deliberately provide gratification for the patient. Within the treatment situation he can be helpful, supportive, and sympathetic while maintaining a therapeutic attitude. This has been discussed in detail elsewhere (Tarachow and Stein, 1967).

FAILURES IN PSYCHOANALYTIC PSYCHOTHERAPY

The specific technical approach and its limitations in psychoanalytic psychotherapy, as described above, indicate two main areas where difficulties might arise in this form of treatment. These areas are those concerned with the transference and the countertransference. Difficulties arise in all forms of psychotherapy in relation to these two factors, but they can be especially troublesome in psychoanalytic psychotherapy. This will be discussed later, after some general considerations concerning failures in psychotherapy.

Much has been written about failures in psychoanalysis and psychotherapy but little has been added to Freud's courageous, thorough, and most clear discussion in "Analysis: Terminable and Interminable," which appeared in 1937. Anna Freud (1968) recently reviewed these considerations and brought them up to date, particularly the resistance of young people to any form of treatment that would ask them to adjust to a form of society they wish to change. Frank (1967) also has discussed this. Hoch's book (1948), *Failures in Psychiatric Treatment* contains many worthwhile contributions to this topic, especially those of Hamilton and Oberndorf. Koren *et al.* (1951), Knight (1941), Reich (1950), and Nunberg (1954) give excellent discussions of dynamic factors involved in failures in psychotherapy, and Wallerstein's comprehensive review (1966) of psychotherapy includes an excellent discussion of results of psychotherapy.

Most of the writers cited have confirmed and elaborated upon the considerations originally cited by Freud and these will be summarized below. They are factors involved in failures in *all* forms of psychotherapy, including analysis.

The general factors leading to failures in all forms of psychotherapy are

1. *Incorrect diagnosis* and, therefore, selecting the wrong form of treatment; this stems from errors in estimating the amount of psychopathology. Treatment is begun with patients who present mild symptoms which later are found to mask very severe disorders often inaccessible to exploratory psychotherapy.

2. *Untoward external conditions*
   a. Where external conditions are so unfavorable that actual gain through remaining sick seems

of greater value than the advantages of good health

    b. Where the attitude of the family supports neurotic (or psychotic) manifestations in the patient

    c. Reality factors—education, class, economic status, and the effect of trauma such as illness and loss

3. *Constitutional factors*—strength of instincts and of conflicts centering around penis envy in women and passive attitudes in men

4. *Unfavorable modifications of the ego*—severe characterological disturbances, and so on

5. *Transference and countertransference*

These are the general factors that most workers feel are involved in failures in psychotherapy. The remainder of the discussion in this paper will be limited to the last two factors listed, transference and countertransference, especially in relation to psychoanalytic psychotherapy.

Transference

The most important point to be made is the one previously stressed: that in psychoanalytic psychotherapy certain aspects of the transference are left uninterpreted and, therefore, this part of the relationship to the therapist is considered as real. It provides support and gratification for the patient but also serves as a major form of resistance.

Repeatedly, in psychoanalytic psychotherapy, the

uninterpreted aspects of the transference will be used by the patient to ask for gratification from the therapist and to resist attempts at self-investigation and working in the treatment. The most skillful handling in the treatment fails to prevent the occurrence of these transference resistances as long as the transference and the countertransference remain uninterpreted.

For example, a young lady came for treatment because of depression and anxiety stemming from difficulties in her relationships with men. She had reached a certain age and felt that she had difficulties which prevented her from having married and establishing good relationships with men. It was reasonably clear that she had expectations that the treatment would somehow do something for her that would help her get married. Great care was taken to point out that there was no guarantee the treatment would help her achieve this, and that all it could do would be to help her understand whatever difficulties stood in her way.

She seemed to accept this, and then we worked for quite some time in the treatment. It became apparent that there were certain other underlying difficulties which needed to be dealt with and that her efforts at seeking out men and establishing good relationships with them were hampered by these underlying difficulties, which centered around her ties with her mother and sister.

When efforts were made to help her see this she became quite angry, and in a rather stormy session she said, "You are just like my father. You do not want me to get married." Here, then, despite all due care in technique, the transference manifested itself. It became very apparent that the transference was being used as a resistance against discussing these other factors which were basic in her difficulties.

To cite another example, a man came for treatment because of anxiety connected with the discovery of a heart condition. In addition, he had many other problems in relation to business, his business associates, and his family. We worked at these very carefully. After a while it became apparent that his participation in the treatment was rather perfunctory. He listened to the interpretations and the comments with cooperation and kindness, you might say, but they really were not making very much of an impression on him. He was not that involved in the treatment. Finally, this was pointed out to him.

He took this as a form of criticism, expressed some anger, and began to speak more freely about certain things. It then became very clear as to how he had used the treatment. He had been informed by his medical doctor that some of the factors that led to his heart attack were emotional, and his coming for treatment was a magic talisman or magic safeguard that would prevent him from having emotional upsets that might lead to further heart attacks. Again, despite careful handling, the patient had used the transference and magic expectations connected with the treatment rather than working through his emotional difficulties.

In both these instances, while some transference interpretations had been made, many of the transference manifestations had been left uninterpreted. Therefore, despite very careful handling, both patients felt that the therapist's efforts were part of a special interest and help he was offering—a fatherly possessiveness in one instance, a mother's magic protectiveness in the other —and they sought this from the therapist rather than working at understanding the underlying conflicts that caused their difficulties.

Countertransference

Turning now to the countertransference, it is well known (Wallerstein, 1966) that this can lead to difficulties in treatment. Freud (1937) particularly cautioned against this, specifically in relation to excessive therapeutic zeal on the part of the therapist. Tarachow (1963) also pointed this out; his description of the various ways in which it can manifest itself is cited above. The therapist's need is to produce results in the treatment rather than to help the patient work something out. This is part of his need for an object relationship with the patient. Obviously, these factors can impose burdens on the patient and lead to failures in the treatment, as illustrated in two brief examples.

A young man with a schizoid personality came for treatment because of depressive symptoms and inability to function. After some time in treatment, during which he had improved considerably but still was unable to work, a wealthy uncle became interested and offered him help in various ways, including a job. The patient began to work and developed a close relationship with the uncle, who gave him many gifts and had him assigned to a well-paying job, and so on. Because the uncle was an unstable person and the help he offered was excessive and unrealistic the therapist attempted to help the patient forgo some of this and try to work out something for himself. The patient reacted with anger to these attempts and abruptly left treatment.

A young woman, with two young children, came for treatment because of depressive symptoms related to her marriage. She was a dependent, narcissistic person with few resources of her own. The marriage was a pathological sado-masochistic one, but the husband, although disturbed, was devoted to the wife. Her own family had been disrupted and, except for the husband, she had no one except a sick mother. The therapist tried to help her adjust to the difficulties in the marriage since she had nowhere else to turn. After some time in treatment, during which she had had several severe depressive episodes in relation to her marital difficulties, she left her husband and left treatment.

In both these instances the therapist had sought to help the patients work something out along the lines he thought best, i.e., by becoming independent and by handling difficult situations better. The patients' needs were along different lines, and in order to achieve these they left treatment. Here therapeutic zeal was one of the major factors in the failure of the treatment.

Another and most important countertransference difficulty occurs when the therapist is unable to see something that is going on in the treatment because of some difficulty of his own. We could cite many examples. A therapist who is unaware of some of the pathological aspects of his competitiveness will not see these in a patient. A therapist who is not aware of certain sadistic, voyeuristic, or other attitudes in himself will not see these in a patient. A therapist can avoid seeing certain conflict areas in the patient that are similar to his own by being either too active or too passive. These are familiar things which need not be elaborated upon.

Freud's (1937) advice in relation to countertransference was for the analyst to repeat an analysis every five years. However, in struggling with these things without going back into analysis every five years, the most important thing, it seems to me, is for the therapist to carefully check on his own attitude in the treatment. Glover (1955), and Tarachow and Stein (1967) have discussed this in detail. If he maintains the right kind of therapeutic attitude and if, in his dealings with the patient, he listens while he has to and intervenes when he has to in proper therapeutic fashion, he will be able to deal with countertransference attitudes insofar as they become available to him in the therapy.

A consistent attempt by the therapist to maintain a proper therapeutic attitude and a constant alertness against any departure from this will do much to help prevent countertransference errors. This is part of an awareness of the conditions and limitations of psychoanalytic psychotherapy as discussed above and will enable the therapist to be more active and limit his interpretations as indicated without creating additional difficulties in the treatment.

Proper utilization of the treatment techniques available within the limitations of psychoanalytic psychotherapy helps the patient move along in the treatment. As described elsewhere (Tarachow and Stein, 1967), the therapist focuses on one area of conflict and bypasses others; he helps the patient strengthen some defenses and lessen or give up others. He makes careful and limited interpretations concerning transference and resistance; these are partial interpretations but they can be quite effective. He helps the patient find proper displacements for certain symptoms and conflicts. He tries to provide ego and superego support and education. And all this is done with the necessary activity but within the framework of the proper therapeutic attitude.

This is the way the therapist proceeds in psychoanalytic psychotherapy, watching for the transference and countertransference manifestations which can so readily occur in this form of treatment. By lessening or eliminating a pathogenic defense in one area, by resolving or working out a derivative—by freeing the ego in one sector, by strengthening defenses in others —the treatment can lead to a rearrangement of the intrapsychic dynamic forces and to improved and sustained better functioning of the patient. His awareness of the limitation of this form of treatment can help him avoid some of the difficulties that lead to failure.

REFERENCES

FRANK, J. D. "Does Psychotherapy Work?" *Internat. Journ. of Psychiatry,* 1967, **3**:153.

FRANK, J. D., and L. H. GLIEDMAN, *et al.* Why Patients Leave Psychotherapy. *Archives Neurol. and Psychiat.*, 1957, **77**:283.

FREUD, A., (1968). "Difficulties in the Path of Psychoanalysis: A Confrontation of Past with Present Viewpoints." New York, International Universities Press.

FREUD, SIGMUND. *Analysis Terminable and Interminable.* Collected Papers, 1937, **V**:316–357. London: Hogarth Press, 1950.

GILL, M. M. Psychoanalysis and Exploratory Psychotherapy. *Journ. Amer. Psychoanal. Ass.*, 1954, **2**:771–797.

GLOVER, E. *The Technique of Psychoanalysis.* New York: International Universities Press, 1955.

GREENSON, R. R. The Working Alliance and the Transference Neurosis. *Psychoanalytic Quarterly*, 1965, **34**:155–181.

KNIGHT, R. P. Evaluation of the Results of Psychoanalytic Therapy. *Amer. J. Psychiat.*, 1941, **98**:434.

KOREN, L., V. GOERTZEL, and M. EVANS, (1951). "The Psychodynamics of Failure in Therapy." *Amer. J. Psychiat.*, **108**: 37–41.

NUNBERG, H. Evaluation of the Results of Psychoanalytic Treatment. *Internat. J. Psychoanal.*, 1954, **35**:2.

RANGELL, L. Psychoanalysis and Dynamic Psychotherapy. *Journ. Amer. Psychoanal. Assn.*, 1954, **2**:771–797.

REICH, A. On the Termination of Analysis. *Internat. J. Psychoanal.*, 1950, **31**:179.

STONE, L. *The Psychoanalytic Situation.* New York: International Universities Press, 1961.

TARACHOW, S. *An Introduction to Psychotherapy.* New York: International Universities Press, 1963.

TARACHOW, S., and A. STEIN. Psychoanalytic Psychotherapy. Chapter XVII, in B. Wolman (ed.), *Psychoanalytic Techniques.* New York: Basic Books, 1967.

WALLERSTEIN, R. S. The Current State of Psychotherapy: Theory, Practice, Research. *Journ. Amer. Psychoanal. Assn.*, 1966, **14**:183–225.

Psychoanalysis and Its Relationship to Socioeconomic and Sociopolitical Change

STANLEY LESSE, M.D., MED.SC.D.

PSYCHOANALYSIS is now approximately seventy years old. In some future evaluation specialists in psychologic medicine will probably designate this period as one in which great progress was made in the understanding of the psychopathologic processes and the dynamics of intrapsychic mechanisms as they pertain to individual patients (Lesse, 1967).

In all probability they will also note with amazement that studies during this period were isolated from an awareness of the broad socioeconomic, sociophilosophic, and sociopolitical currents that have dominated psychotherapists and patients alike. It would appear that the sweeping political, economic, and philosophic changes of the last seventy years have had relatively little influence on the development of theoretic formulations of psychoanalytic techniques, as evidenced by a review of the literature or a study of curricula of the various schools of psychoanalysis.

Many readers will no doubt protest vehemently at these remarks. Some neo-Freudians will stress the work of Horney or Sullivan as evidence of a broader social awareness than that postulated by Freud. While such statements are true in general, strictly speaking the neo-Freudian conceptualizations are narrow expansions of the basic Freudian focus on intrapsychic mechanisms. Alfred Adler, who was rejected by Freud and by most of Freud's followers, had the broadest conceptualization of the interrelationships between the individual and the community. However, he too failed to appreciate the effects of sweeping economic and political trends on the individual. It is a sad commentary that most of us first, second, or third generation followers of the founders of psychoanalysis have developed psychoanalysis in a veritable vacuum as far as effective awareness of these trends is concerned.

While the world is always in a state of revolutionary sociologic and technologic change, the last half century, particularly the last twenty years, has been characterized by a rapid acceleration in the rate of change that has occurred technologically, socioeconomically, sociopolitically, and sociophilosophically (Lesse and Wolf, 1966). The promise for the future is that this acceleration will continue to increase in the coming years. Institutions that were relatively stable for decades and even centuries are either drastically altered or are facing the necessity to alter if they are to survive. We are at crossroads in almost every area in life. In the not too distant future our civilization is likely to show patterns of development radically different from those we recognize today. Psychotherapies of all types must keep pace with these changes if we are not to be hampered by concepts and practices stemming from an earlier revolutionary period; there is, indeed, nothing as stale and outmoded as an old revolution.

The obligation to be completely aware of a passing scene is especially important for those who teach, since the students of today will be practitioners, teachers, and leaders of our profession in the beginning of the twenty-first century. In order adequately to prepare students of any type psychotherapy for the rapidly changing scene radically new conceptualizations of teaching and practice must be devised—conceptualizations that focus upon the relationships between individual dynamics and group sociodynamics projected in terms of a historic perspective in which future cultural-technologic patterns are anticipated (Lesse, 1968).

SOCIAL BACKGROUND OF CURRENT THEORIES AND TECHNIQUES

Our current psychoanalytic and psychoanalytically oriented techniques were born in late Victorian Europe in a culture in which the pent-up energies of the bourgeoisie dominated the economic, cultural, and in most instances the political trends (Schick, 1964a). While some socialist ideas were stirring, it was individualism that was extolled as never before. Private property was held sacred. Nationalist feelings ran high. It was a time of marching bands and marching soldiers. To be an avowed patriot and to express love of the fatherland were common and chic.

The family unit was strong. The guiding hand was

that of a patriarchal father; his image was dominant and usually unchallenged. The great struggle of that time was still for food, shelter, and clothing. Luxuries were not as yet taken for granted. Factories were, in the main, small, and mass production was as yet the exception. Hand labor with an emphasis on quality workmanship and services was still the order of the day. Mass production began to appear on a larger scale, particularly in heavy industry. The ugliness of labor exploitation and the abuse of child labor were just beginning to stir a poorly informed populace. The craftsman, who was to dominate the early labor movement, had a great emotional investment in his work, for his work was a prime source of pride and pleasure.

Expansionism and colonialism were considered healthy and just causes. The "white man's burden" was to spread European culture throughout the world. This concept prevailed with an air of romance and adventure heralded by the sounds of trumpets, marching youth, and applauding women. The telegraph was still the prime means of long-distance communication. The telephone was as yet the property of the few. By current standards, transportation was relatively slow. Warfare was still a combat between individual men or small units, if one uses today's armies as a standard.

Throughout this scene, the individual was in his ascendency, the bourgeoisie as a group replaced the aristocracy as the dominant force, and legislative rule replaced autocracy in most Western countries.

These trends, together with many other ethnic, philosophic, and cultural forces that were peculiar to a decadent and dying Austro-Hungarian Empire, became fused into a mass of energy in Vienna, where, amidst a flame of new literature, poetry, music, and philosophy, the theories and practices of Freud, Adler, Stekel, and others were born (Schick, 1964b). These men were a product of their times and culture, and their theories and techniques reflected and focused upon the individual. (Adler is included in this statement for, though he had a strong social awareness, his basic theoretic formulations and techniques also stressed the individual.)

It was from this era and background that today's basic psychotherapeutic techniques were spawned. Classic psychoanalytic procedures and, indeed, the neo-Freudian schools as well as the schools started by Adler and Jung, all stress the individual's awareness of himself. They uniquely condition the patient to adjust to a socioeconomic and sociopolitical setting in which he must care for himself and his family both economically and socially.

PRIME FACTORS IN PSYCHOANALYTIC TECHNIQUES

It has been assumed traditionally by the teachers and practitioners of the many schools of psychoanalytic and psychoanalytically oriented psychotherapy that an understanding by the patient of the psychodynamic mechanisms pertaining to his particular problems is the key to emotional maturation and adaptive functioning. In keeping with this belief, the many schools of psychotherapy have evolved and then refined specific interpretations which many of us have chanted and rechanted, at times as if they were part of a liturgy. However, despite this stereotypy of interpretation, there is no evidence that any one school of psychotherapy has had better results than another school.

The reasons for the similarity in results obtained by these schools lie in the fact that the basic techniques employed by all of them are very similar. The psychodynamic formulations, the frequency and duration of treatment, the position of the patient, the amount of verbal communication between the patient and therapist, and/or the question of group therapy versus individual therapy admittedly may have important effects on the outcome of treatment. However, these are not the prime factors in producing psychic change and they do not have the greatest influence on the final results obtained by the patients.

The prime factors in all of the various psychoanalytic and psychoanalytically oriented psychotherapies are those fundamental aspects indivisibly built into the techniques that stress the individual patient's awareness of himself, those factors that stress the "I" and "me" and "mine." A strong conditioned reflex mechanism is automatically established by all of these procedures, a conditioned reflex that is "I-" and "me-" oriented.

This is accomplished in all dynamically oriented psychotherapeutic procedures by the very use of such techniques as free association, retrospective analysis of the child–parent relationship, the detailed ontologic reconstruction of the patient's psychic development, the release of unconscious material through dreams, fantasies and slips of the tongue, and the working through of the transference relationship. These and the other techniques basic to dynamically oriented psychotherapy are the prime and most important factors in all psychoanalytic or psychoanalytically oriented psychotherapies. These procedures emphasize the patient's awareness of himself and they overwhelmingly focus upon "I was, I am, I will be."

Even in relationship to group activity, this type of psychotherapeutic orientation prepares the patient to function as an individual in a group. In a group setting, a large number of such "I-" oriented patients function as a collective of "I's" in which the individual ego takes precedence over the "we" (the group ego). With this type of therapeutic orientation, the individual always remains more important than the group "I" always remains more important than the "we".

As such, psychoanalytic and psychoanalytically oriented therapies are uniquely suited to prepare patients psychologically to adapt and function in cultures that require the individual to protect himself and his family and that place the image of the individual on a pedestal. In a contrary vein, these treatment techniques inadequately or even adversely prepare the patient to function in a culture in which individualism is not extolled or where it is deprecated. The benefits and adverse aspects of the concepts of psychoanalytically oriented procedures can be illustrated by their application to patients drawn from various socioeconomic groups in the United States and from their application to patients in the Soviet Union.

APPLICATION OF THE PSYCHOTHERAPIES IN THE UNITED STATES

The United States has a very broad socioeconomic structure. At one end of the spectrum is a group of men and women the members of which are completely dependent upon themselves for their financial security. Their stability and the stability of their families depend entirely upon how much each of them can earn as an individual. Many receive no protection from the government, such as accident and health compensation, unemployment insurance, or social security. The economic protection they require to cover current emergencies and future contingencies must be obtained on their own initiative. If they do not anticipate and provide for these contingencies, or if they are financially unable to afford the various protection plans that can be purchased, they and their families may be submerged at times of crises such as economic failure, illness, or death. In the United States and in most European countries, since the end of World War II, this group has been shrinking rapidly. However, it still includes a large number of persons gathered mainly from the various professions.

This fading segment of individualistically oriented society is the fast disappearing remnant of a scheme of life epitomized at the turn of the twentieth century in the United States as the "Protestant Ethic," a concept that was most cogently summarized in 1908 by Henry Clews. This ethic, in its present form, worshipped free competition and private property, and extolled economic survival of the fittest. It preached that success was due entirely to one's natural qualities and not to chance. In cavalier fashion it stated that a man rightfully deserved whatever riches he gained by his individual enterprise (Clews, 1908). This represented an extreme view, but the precepts of this segment of Western culture are applicable in a modified fashion to all individuals who are basically dependent upon self-employment.

Dynamic, analytically oriented psychotherapies are uniquely suited to patients such as these, when they decompensate psychically. These therapies reinforce the ego capacities of such patients in a manner that prepares them to return to an individually oriented milieu and to the particular type of adaptive struggle that is part and parcel of this milieu. The techniques themselves, for the reasons already indicated, supplemented by various interpretations pointedly interjected by the therapist, literally transfuse the patient's "I" orientation and send him back to his socioeconomic battle charged with the kind of fuel and ammunition required for his particular type of adaptive struggle. Again, it is primarily the technique and not the quality or frequency of interpretation that is responsible for change. At best, the interpretations tend to reinforce that which was accomplished by the basic aspects of the technique.

It is a paradoxic but nevertheless true observation that our increasingly complex industrial and social scene has generated an avalanche of necessary social legislation which in itself has increased rather than decreased the stresses faced by the individualist. The individualist is literally legislating himself out of existence and rapidly becoming an anachronism.

The socioeconomic and sociopolitical stresses currently faced by the professional man and individual entrepreneur are of such magnitude that our dynamically oriented psychotherapeutic techniques are not equal, in many instances, to the rehabilitative task that is required. It would appear that the increasing cultural demands may be outstripping our psychotherapeutic abilities in this segment of our population.

In contrast to this fading group of individualists, there are in the United States several "socialistically oriented groups" (if one uses the term socialistic in a very broad fashion). These are of three types:

1. Groups of persons employed by large corporations (organization men).
2. Groups of workers in industry, belonging to craft and industrial unions.
3. Groups of persons employed by the local, state, and federal governments.

The so-called "organization man" works in a type of socialistically oriented society, if one uses the term socialist to mean collective ownership as well as government ownership, a concept that has great merit. It is a type of collective that is the unique product of a successful capitalist system and it would appear that the organization is a transitional stage on the road to a socialist, socioeconomic scheme. Karl Marx, though he was quite accurate in some of his predictions with regard to the decline of bourgeoisie and the ascendency of the proletariat in a capitalist society, was so blinded by his neuroticisms and hatred of capitalism that he could not conceive of successful capitalism in a democratic republic and therefore could not comprehend or predict the appearance of the organization as a peaceful, nonviolent stepping-stone to socialism.

The organization man has different appearances depending upon how high in the hierarchy he has climbed. At all levels the organization becomes a protecting parental figure in the unconscious of the employee. It becomes the all-kind, the all-knowing father, and the employee commonly refers to the organization in terms of "we" and "our." He cannot conceive that the organization would ever do him harm or that it would fail to protect him. His status in the world depends upon the success of the organization. In contrast to many of the individually employed persons described above, employees of large corporations at all levels are protected by government compensation and retirement plans. Most employees also have supplementary free medical insurance and a pension plan. In the higher echelons these pension plans are often super generous, to say the least.

The organization men at the executive and junior executive levels have a falsified image of themselves. They consider themselves highly individualistic beings. Indeed, it is these same "socialized leaders" of the organization that fill the press with statements extolling individualism. This is as incongruous as if the Premier of the U.S.S.R. was to praise private ownership. The executive in a large corporation has much more in common with the executive in a large union than he has with the professional man or the owner of a small plant or business.

However, psychoanalytically oriented techniques are applicable in the management of patients drawn from the executive ranks of the organization. This is particularly true where there is some sociologic awareness on the part of the therapists. The executive and junior executive demonstrate a peculiar blend of individualism and group dependency. Most commonly it is the failure in the executive organization man's ability to function as an individualist—which is at times necessary—that causes him to decompensate psychically and to seek psychiatric help.

The psychoanalytic psychotherapies reinforce the executive's capacity to function on an individualistic basis. They emphasize and strengthen the executive's awareness of himself, his individual ego in contrast to his group ego. This psychic reorganization, which in this instance is a form of ego transfusion, is necessary for one holding a high office in a large hierarchically ordered organization.

In contrast to the executive, the employees at the bottom of this hierarchically ordered organizational structure become a mass of psychosocial similarities without individual identification. They are completely dependent on the organization and on government protection for their security. Individualism at this level is frowned upon and could lead to ostracism and loss of jobs. Intensive psychoanalytic psychotherapy would appear to be contraindicated in many of these patients and is not the treatment of choice in many others.

The author has observed several such patients in whom psychoanalytic psychotherapy fired off or stimulated the patients' self-awareness to the point that they could not readjust to the organization. However, they did not have sufficient intellectual ability or ego strength to advance in the organization, nor did they have the ability to leave the organization and function in a competitive society as individual entrepreneurs. This is the real danger in the application of psychodynamically oriented psychotherapy to patients who have limited capacities and who must readjust and submerge themselves in the group.

That which has been described for the organization man is also very applicable to government employees, particularly those in the lower echelons. However, the senior career civil service employee rarely manifests the degree of individual self-awareness or self-expression that is characteristic of most organization men in high executive capacities. The ego of the long-term civil servant becomes irrevocably submerged and diffused into the group ego and rarely does it become revitalized, despite promotion to high office.

Workers in organized labor are completely dependent on the union and upon government agencies for their personal security. They do not determine their own economic and social progress. Their very being is integrated into the union, and while they may at times debate the relative merits of different labor leaders they are pulled along inexorably by group opinion and group action. The unionized worker looks upon the union leader and the government as the good fathers, while the employer and the organization executive have become the bogeymen.

On the other hand, the labor leader has far more in common emotionally with the organization executive than he has with the average laborer. The sources of his emotional difficulties are very similar to those of the executive.

If the average laborer too forcefully demonstrates signs of individualistic pursuits, he courts isolation and even ostracism. In such instances, unless the laborer has the intellectual and emotional capacities and the drive to function apart from the group, the psychotherapist by the use of psychoanalytic techniques does this type of patient a disservice by arousing or teasing individual capacities that are inadequate to permit the worker to stand alone.

PSYCHOTHERAPY IN THE SOVIET UNION

The society in the Soviet Union was selected as the example of a long established socialist system. The Bolshevik type of socialism is more than a political philosophy; it is a way of life. Although it professes to be a philosophy that has broad applications, it has gone further and has taken on the aura of a religion.

Communism stresses that the individual is important only as a part of the group and has strength and security only to the extent that he is part of the group. Individualism, which remains an object of admiration in many circles in the United States, is deprecated in the Communist society. It exposes the individual who indulges in such activity to scorn and indeed may cause him difficulties with the authorities.

Psychotherapy in the U.S.S.R., by emphasizing the patient's relationship to his environment, has little resemblance to the techniques employed in the Western countries (Lesse, 1958). The Soviet patient's difficulties are interpreted as being due to his conflicts with his environment. By techniques of persuasion, suggestion, and interpretation, the psychotherapist reemphasizes the patient's role in the local and national group. The therapist stresses the fact that the patient is a part of a group and that he derives great benefits and security only from the collective strength of the group. Unconscious conflict is considered to be of relatively little importance.

Psychoanalysis would be contraindicated in a patient in a communist community. It might well hinder the patient's capacities to adapt to this type of culture. On the one hand, communist philosophy stresses that the individual is part of the group and has importance, meaning, and security only to the extent that he is part of the group. On the other hand, psychoanalytic psychotherapy, as I have outlined above, emphasizes the patient's individualism and thereby would ill prepare the psychiatric patient for his return to his role in the

Soviet group, a group which would disparage or even punish him for expressions of individualism.

CONCLUSIONS

During the past year officials and representatives of the two major psychoanalytic associations in the United States have realistically pointed up the incompatibilities between current psychoanalytic theory and technique and the current social scene. This awareness of the anachronistic aspects of psychoanalysis is only the first step. There must be a probing investigation that will be in depth as to whether many of our time-honored psychodynamic conceptualizations and psychoanalytic practices are little more than ecclesiastic-like dogma and ritualized habit.

It has not been my intention to deprecate the importance of the intrapsychic aspects of emotional illness which has been learned through psychoanalytic methods or to play down the necessity to understand the psychodynamic mechanisms. Also, I did not intend to imply that the therapist's interpretations to the patient were of small moment. It has been my purpose here to emphasize the fact that socioeconomic and sociopolitical factors must be considered in the selection of specific psychotherapeutic techniques. The very nature of a psychotherapeutic technique will aid or hinder a patient in his adaptation to a given economic or political milieu.

In viewing the future role of psychoanalysis, consideration must be given to the likelihood that in the not too distant future the best that psychiatrists and psychotherapists might accomplish will be prevention of psychic disorders. To be most effective, prophylactic measures of a psychologic nature must be indivisibly incorporated in the sociopolitical and socioeconomic system in which one lives. It may well be that optimally all psychiatrists, psychotherapists, and social scientists in the future will be "social psychiatrists" or "psychiatric sociologists"—terms implying that both groups will understand the relationships between sociodynamics and individual psychodynamics. Heretofore all social revolutions have been hit-or-miss propositions in regard to whether the projected political or economic systems would be psychically beneficial to the individual man. The world is becoming too crowded and technologically too advanced to be run by men who do not comprehend the relationships between social forces and psychodynamic mechanisms. The psychotherapist of the not too distant future in his radically changed image of a psychosociologist will have just as great a role to play as political scientist as he will have as diagnostician and therapist.

REFERENCES

CLEWS, H. *Fifty years in Wall Street.* New York: Irving Publishing, 1908.

LESSE, S. Current clinical and research trends in Soviet psychiatry. *Amer. J. Psychiat.,* 1958, 114:1018–1022.

LESSE, S. Psychotherapy—an apocalyptic view. Editorial. *Amer. J. Psychotherapy,* 1967, 21:561–564.

LESSE, S. Patients, therapists and socioeconomics, in S. Lesse (ed.), *An Evaluation of the Results of the Psychotherapies.* Springfield, Ill.: Charles C. Thomas, 1968.

LESSE, S. and W. WOLF. An exploration of the basic determinants and trends of medicine in our future society. *Amer. J. Psychotherapy*, 1966, **20**:206–227.

SCHICK, A. The cultural background of Adler's and Freud's work. *Amer. J. Psychotherapy*, 1964, **18**:7–24(a).

SCHICK, A. The relationships between socioeconomic and sociopolitical practices and psychotherapeutic techniques. *Amer. J. Psychotherapy*, 1964, **18**:574–583(b).

WHYTE, W. H. *The Organizational Man*. New York: Simon & Schuster, 1956.

Ferment in Psychoanalysis and Psychoanalytic Psychotherapy

HANS H. STRUPP, PH.D.

NEED FOR RESEARCH

THE PROBLEM of success and failure in psychotherapy (under which I subsume psychoanalysis) entered a new phase in the 1960s, some of whose salient features may be briefly characterized as follows:

1. In the research literature—here it is important to mention that serious research in this area has increasingly become the province of American psychologists, with some help from colleagues in Great Britain and on the continent—one finds a growing disenchantment with psychoanalysis and psychotherapy based on psychoanalytic principles. The arguments have essentially followed this pattern:

a. Psychoanalytic psychotherapy in general and orthodox psychoanalysis in particular are hopelessly inefficient methods for coping with the inexhaustible reservoir of human misery for which the services of psychotherapists are needed. The available professional manpower is grossly inadequate and it is demonstrably impossible to narrow the gap in any significant way by training a larger number of therapists.

b. This form of therapy and its variants has always been and remains restricted to a narrow segment of the population who are intelligent, affluent, verbal, psychological-minded, and endowed with other superior qualifications. Conversely, the vast majority of people who need help neither meet these qualifications nor can they afford the services of a highly trained psychotherapist even if they meet the criteria and therapists were available. Thus it follows inexorably that other methods—cheaper, more efficient, less demanding—must be developed. Indeed, a wide variety of such techniques have been developed and are already widely applied. Most prominently here are techniques derived from learning principles. The avowed aim is "behavior modification" (a term which has begun to supersede "psychotherapy"), which is now regarded as encompassing such "traditional" methods as psychoanalysis, client-centered therapy, and other forms of one-to-one therapy in an office setting. The enormous appeal of the former methods derives in part from these considerations: (1) They are applicable to a considerably larger segment of the population, including mental hospital patients, lower-class individuals, and many others; (2) they are said to be more efficient and far less expensive; (3) they often do not require a high level of therapeutic skill, so that subprofessionals and even laymen can function in the therapeutic role; (4) they are claimed to be more effective than the so-called traditional methods.

2. The issue of therapeutic effectiveness has become the prime criterion of any approach and the touchstone of its popularity and value. This issue was forcefully brought to the fore by Eysenck (1952), who

alleged that psychotherapists in general have failed to demonstrate the efficacy of their procedures. While his initial argument, buttressed by data open to other interpretations besides the ones he chose, emphasized the absence of strong positive evidence, he and a growing host of followers have more recently asserted the superiority of behaviorally oriented methods. They have also presented a considerable body of empirical data to substantiate their points. I shall presently discuss and analyze in detail a representative study purporting to compare "traditional" psychotherapy with "behavior modification." This kind of research is frequently cited as demonstrating conclusively the superiority of the newer approaches to psychotherapy. Whatever the merits of these therapeutic techniques and the associated research, their impact on the field as a whole, notably through university training programs, has been extraordinary.

3. Whereas research-oriented psychologists (and a few psychiatrists) have labored to expand the therapeutic armamentarium along the lines sketched above, tested new approaches, conducted laboratory research to shed light on the psychological mechanisms at work, published a vast number of more or less well controlled studies, and in general extolled empiricism as the ultimate standard for any therapeutic endeavor, psychoanalysts and other dynamically oriented therapists have essentially conducted "business as usual." I believe this judgment is substantially correct despite the emergence of a certain number of research studies dealing with the process and outcome of this form of

therapy, developments along the lines of group psychotherapy, community mental health, brief psychotherapy, and so on, and a mild interest in empirical evidence. In the large metropolitan areas like New York
or Los Angeles there is a concentration of analytically
oriented psychotherapists, typically organized in
tightly knit professional groups, whose patients are re-
cruited from the upper middle class and seen in intensive treatment for several years. Most of these therapists show little interest in research, the egregious
needs of society at large, the extent to which their therapeutic interventions are effective, or ways in which
they might be improved.

Lest the foregoing be understood as a wholesale indictment of a professional group many of whose members I hold in high esteem, let me point out that I
make these statements out of a sense of profound re-
gret. By turning their collective back, as it were, upon
serious and open inquiry, by discouraging free communication with other behavioral sciences, by taking
for granted a set of procedures which have undergone
basically little change over the years and treating them
as gospel truth, by being insufficiently self-critical and
preponderantly unresponsive to social needs, analytically oriented psychotherapists have abdicated important responsibilities. Largely because of this failure
—not because of demonstrated therapeutic ineffectiveness!—Freud's significant contributions are
being overshadowed and in the foreseeable future may
indeed be eclipsed by techniques which in terms of
psychological sophistication, clinical penetration, and

humaneness represent a retreat from a hard-won bastion (Strupp, 1968).

CRITERIA OF CURE

The clinician, typically, is convinced of the worthiness of his therapeutic endeavors and, like Freud, is unimpressed by "statistics." A large majority of patients, too, feel benefited by their psychotherapeutic experience. To an important degree, the question revolves around one's definition of "improvement." As I have attempted to show elsewhere (Strupp, 1963), the kinds of improvement psychoanalysts are talking about are vastly different from the criteria Eysenck (1952, 1961) invoked, but in either case the criteria must be *specifiable*.

If a behavior therapist is willing to consider the alleviation of a snake phobia in an otherwise well-functioning personality a "cure," this is his privilege, and he cannot be challenged by other therapists who may prefer to work toward different objectives, nor can he challenge them. But it is incumbent upon all therapists to be explicit about their goals. In this connection, Knight's (1941) criteria may be too vague to serve as guidelines, but they are specifiable in principle. (His major rubrics were: (1) disappearance of presenting symptoms; (2) real improvement in mental functioning; (3) improved reality adjustment.) The scientific community and the public have a right to know the rules by which the therapeutic game is played, and they are entitled to pass a value judgment on them.

Analytic therapists, it seems to me, have devoted insufficient attention to this problem and in general shrugged off the researcher's insistence upon hard-core evidence as indicative of ignorance or ulterior motives. If it is true, as Szasz (1967) asserts, that the kind of learning in psychoanalysis is entirely different from that occurring in behavior therapy and if it is true that the former is principally concerned with increasing the patient's sphere of autonomy rather than alleviating his symptoms, there must exist *some* criteria by which such changes can be judged. These criteria must be communicable and at least in some way they must refer to aspects of the person's behavior.

I contend that the issue is a legitimate one and it can be ignored only at the risk of ultimate disastrous effects. Some of these are already becoming apparent. The chaos pervading the entire area of psychotherapy and psychotherapy research to which several authors (Colby, 1964; Matarazzo, 1965) have called attention is at least partly attributable to the failure to specify the precise nature of the operations which are designed to achieve a given objective in a particular person. Too often, unfortunately, therapists have acted as if the problem did not exist, or as if it did not merit their attention. We cannot negate the simple fact that a patient comes to a psychotherapist because of a "problem" for which he is seeking a solution. No matter how the problem is conceptualized or attacked, the end result must be a form of change demonstrable by the scientific rules of evidence. For this reason I have omitted from consideration a large number of "humanistic" or "existentialistic" approaches to psychotherapy which have achieved prominence in this country in recent years. Many of these appear to have a mystic or semi-religious flavor, and their proponents show little interest in, or openly disparage, a scientific attitude toward personality and behavior change.

The therapist is entirely justified in specifying his goals and the criteria he is willing to accept. Other members of the community may consider these goals unimportant, incommensurate with the expended effort, impractical, or trivial. These are value judgments —as is true of all outcome criteria in the final analysis. But once the therapist has stated his goals and his techniques, he must abide by the rules and have the fruits of his work judged accordingly. I am convinced that if concerted efforts were made along these lines, the showing of psychoanalytic therapy would be vastly more favorable than the existing literature suggests, but at the same time I am prepared to admit that personal opinion (even if augmented by clinical experience) will not decide the issue.

For an incisive discussion of the problem of evidence in psychoanalytic research see Wolman (1964). According to him, outcome criteria (praxiological propositions), while involving value judgments, need not be excluded from natural science. However, "an agreed-upon norm of mental health is a prerequisite for any sensible research in psychoanalytic or any other method of treatment. . . . In the absence of objective criteria, any criticism of psychoanalytic technique lacks objectivity. The only way out is to accept at least temporarily Freud's criteria and to ask the question whether psychoanalytic, classic, or modified procedure brings the hoped-for results." (page 728). The need for agreed-upon criteria is clearly urgent.

To elaborate on the *choice* of criteria: In this country we find a strong emphasis on behavioral criteria, epitomized by the question, Does the patient *act* differently after psychotherapy? Following psychotherapy, he may interact differently with his spouse, his children, his boss, he may become more assertive with people in general, engage in activities he previously avoided, etc. To be sure, these are exceedingly important indices, and not only because they are open to observation, measurement, and verification. I agree that any form of psychotherapy worthy of the name must be capable of producing such changes (or inducing the patient to make them). But there is also a wide area of *internal* changes which are notoriously difficult to specify, observe, and measure. Investigators committed to a behavioristic orientation and society may not consider them important, but until therapists working toward internal changes become more articulate about their goals and subject them to systematic study, their assertions that the patient becomes more mature, self-reliant, independent, and more skillful in handling interpersonal situations will be ignored. To this end it will be necessary to place greater weight on the patient's own testimony, as our research group (together with some other researchers) has attempted to do, and a bridge must be built between subjective (necessarily fallible) and objective data. But in principle internal changes are as real as behavioral ones, although one's personal preference may be for one rather than the other.

Consider an outstanding characteristic of neurosis, regardless of whether it is viewed as an "illness" or as a "problem in living." I am referring to the ubiquity of intense suffering, misery, anxiety, hopelessness, and despair. Novelists, poets, and philosophers have been articulate about these feelings, which defy quantification but are as undeniably real to anyone who has experienced them or has the capacity to empathize with them as anything in the world.

Like any pain, neurotic suffering is a subjective state which cannot be captured by behavioral measures no matter how sophisticated they may be. To assess it in any meaningful way we must rely on the patient's testimony. But how can one compare a person's feelings today with those he experienced last year? How can one compare one person's pain with someone else's? Feelings fluctuate; they are elusive; people are suggestible; and their testimony may be highly unreliable. In the face of these dilemmas, the behaviorist throws up his hands and turns to "behavioral indicators" which are observable by others and concerning which a consensus can be reached. But do we have a right to ignore salient aspects of a person's life simply because we have found no effective ways of measuring them? To reiterate my thesis, it appears that the chaotic state of outcome statistics from psychotherapy is at least partially due to the researcher's inability or unwillingness to recognize this problem. It is symptomatic of our time that it is not often discussed.

To be sure, changes in feeling states often accompany changes in behavior but there is no one-to-one relationship, nor can one serve as a substitute for the other. Every therapist and patient can cite abundant examples of behaviors which remain unchanged throughout therapy, but a given situation may be perceived and reacted to differently as a result of therapeutic work. What value are we to place on such changes? As I suggested, if a form of psychotherapy never or rarely produced changes in the patient's overt behavior there would be considerable ground for skepticism about its utility; however, it seems inordinately narrow to restrict evaluations of psychotherapy to changes in overt behavior. Nevertheless, therapists do not have the right to label as "therapeutic" *any* procedure or activity they wish to dignify by this label. In fact, the term "psychotherapy" is used far too loosely and often has little specific meaning. The burden of proof is upon the therapist, not upon the critic. This does not mean that the therapist is obligated to play the game by rules the critics might impose, particularly if they are based on ignorance of the therapist's concerns and objectives.

To illustrate my points I propose to discuss two studies of psychotherapy, the first purporting to demonstrate the superiority of behavioral approaches over "traditional" methods. It is my contention that it achieves its objective only in a highly circumscribed sense and at the expense of defining psychotherapy in a very special way. The second investigation, conducted by my research group, focuses on internal changes experienced by patients who underwent psychotherapy of a more conventional sort. Neither study *proves* the effectiveness of psychotherapy as a technique for helping solve real problems in living, nor does it demonstrate that one approach is better than another. My purpose is to highlight the assertion that (1) the term psychotherapy as used today is a multifaceted conglomerate with fuzzy meanings; (2) as long as there is no reasonable consensus about methods, objectives, and outcomes, comparative studies will remain largely meaningless; and (3) the effectiveness of psychotherapy is largely a definitional problem involving value judgments about the kinds of outcomes a given investigator (or the public at large) deems worthwhile.

A Comparative Outcome Study

A study by Paul (1966) is often cited as strong evidence for the superiority of behavior therapy over "traditional" approaches. Singling out anxiety as a research focus, Paul was interested in examining the relative efficiency of therapeutic procedures derived from "disease" and "learning" models in the treatment of anxiety in public-speaking situations. Specifically, the study was designed to compare insight-oriented psychotherapy with modified systematic desensitization.

Measures included a sizable battery of self-report tests, autonomic indices of anxiety and physiological arousal, and a behavioral check list of performance anxiety.

The therapists were five experienced practitioners representing a mixture of the Freudian, neo-Freudian, and Rogerian orientation. They were paid for their services by the investigator.

Three methods of treatment were employed: (1) Insight-oriented psychotherapy, described as consisting of traditional interview procedures aimed at insight; (2) modified systematic desensitization based on the procedures advocated by Wolpe (1958), including prominently progressive relaxation and desensitization to anxiety-provoking stimuli; and (3) attention-placebo, a procedure administered by the same therapists for the purpose of determining the extent of improvement from nonspecific treatment effects, such as expectation of relief, attention and interest on the part of the therapist, and "faith." Subjects ingested a placebo pill, represented to them as a "fast-acting tranquilizer," and underwent a task described as very stressful.

Two control groups were employed, the first being a no-treatment classroom control, which followed the same procedures as the experimental groups except for the treatment itself; and a no-contact classroom control, which took the pre-treatment and follow-up battery but otherwise did not participate in the investigation.

Subjects were undergraduate college students enrolled in a public-speaking course. A letter accompanying the pre-treatment battery which was administered to 710 students stated that the study was designed to determine "which people benefit most from various types of psychological procedures used to treat anxieties." About half of the original group expressed a desire for treatment. After screening, subjects identified as highly anxious were assigned to the various groups. Each treatment group comprised 15 subjects, the control groups 22 and 29 respectively. These individuals appeared to be "good bets" for psychotherapy in terms of motivation, degree of disturbance, intelligence, age, social class, and so on.

Following a pre-treatment test speech, which was preceded by the stress measures, the students were given an interview. They then entered therapy with their respective therapists. Each person had five hours of individual therapy over a period of six weeks. Upon termination, they gave a post-treatment test speech, accompanied by the same measures.

It is noteworthy that the five therapists administered all forms of therapy, a procedure which controlled for therapist differences. However, since they were not familiar with the desensitization treatment, they were given special training. It may be assumed that they felt more at home with the "traditional" procedures they ordinarily used in their therapeutic work.

The results, based on extensive statistical analyses, showed systematic desensitization to be consistently superior to the other methods. No differences were found between the effects of insight-oriented psychotherapy and the nonspecific effects of the attention placebo treatment, although both groups showed greater anxiety reduction than the no-treatment control groups. Follow-up studies showed that the therapeutic gains were maintained and that no symptom substitution had occurred. On the basis of his results Paul concluded that "treatment based upon a learning model is most effective in alleviating anxiety of a social-evaluation nature" (page 99) and that "the bulk of the evidence in the literature favors the superiority of direct treatment based upon principles of learning over traditional 'depth' approaches" (page 76).

The study is a good example of a contemporary investigation of psychotherapy which reveals careful attention to problems of measurement and control. However, does it prove what it set out to prove?

1. *Are the patients "real" patients?* As already mentioned, this is in part a definitional problem. Paul was certainly at liberty to define the term as he did; however, it may be argued that his subjects actually had little in common with persons who typically apply for psychotherapy to an outpatient clinic or to a private practitioner. They were presumably well-functioning young adults who saw no need for psychotherapy prior to being approached by the investigator. True, the evidence showed that they experienced "public-speaking anxiety," but it is questionable whether this constituted a serious problem in their lives. Certainly, they did not see it as an incapacitating symptom for which they actively sought help.

There were other differences: Whereas the bona fide neurotic patient must take the first step in enlisting professional help, the students in this study were *offered* psychotherapy. Little inconvenience or sacrifice in terms of money or time was involved, and they were spared the painful decision often faced by prospective patients whether or not to admit defeat and seek help. There is little evidence that these students were suffering in any sense of the word. Besides their being *invited* to participate, the professional services were provided as a courtesy. In sum, it appears that the students were more comparable to subjects participating in a psychological experiment than they were to patients seeking help for neurotic problems.

2. *Does the study provide a fair test of the relative merits of different forms of psychotherapy?* In order to examine this question it is necessary to consider the goals of the two forms of therapy being compared. Insight-oriented psychotherapy was defined solely in terms of "traditional interview procedures" used by these therapists in their daily work. "With this approach," states Paul, "the therapist attempts to reduce anxiety by helping the client to gain 'insight' into the bases and interrelationships of his problem" (page 18). While the therapists asserted that insight was an important therapeutic goal in their work, there is no evidence that they focused specifically in the five hours allotted to them upon the reduction of the symptom defined as public-speaking anxiety, nor would one ordinarily expect them to do so.

Evidently, the five therapists were given no instructions about the therapeutic goals the investigator had postulated nor was an effort made to insure uniformity of the therapeutic procedure. It is safe to infer that each therapist proceeded very differently, a problem which was not adequately solved by administering to them a check list intended to assess the frequency with which they used a series of techniques *in general*. It appears that "traditional insight-oriented therapy" was inadequately defined and that the therapists were a rather heterogeneous group, as shown also by the mixture of theoretical orientations they professed.

While some therapists subscribing to a dynamic orientation specialize in brief or goal-limited psychotherapy, no evidence was presented that the therapists in this study typically worked along those lines. As is well known, most dynamic therapists are not primarily concerned with the alleviation of an isolated symptom and they do not accept patients on that basis. Paul apparently induced them to work toward his goals rather than toward their own. Many therapists would have refused such an assignment.

The dynamic psychotherapies (and this is true also of client-centered therapy) are generally concerned with "real" patients, that is, individuals motivated to seek help for problems in interpersonal relations and affects they experience as troublesome. Contrary to the behavior therapist who focuses on specific symptoms which he views as "the problem," dynamic therapists regard symptoms as manifestations of a neurotic process which permeates the person's total functioning. Their therapeutic efforts, therefore, are aimed at helping the patient gain a different view of himself and achieve greater mastery, independence, and autonomy. To be sure, all therapists hope that as a result of their interventions the patient's symptoms will abate and that he will feel more comfortable with himself and others. Behavior therapists, of course, argue that the modification of specific behaviors will achieve the same end (besides doing it more efficiently), and that dynamic therapists have failed to adduce substantive evidence in favor of pervasive personality changes. But what constitutes acceptable evidence?

As I have suggested, this question concerns the criteria of change or improvement one is willing to accept. A specific symptom, as well as changes in a symptom, can be defined with far greater precision than changes in the person's self-concept, subjective comfort, competence in interpersonal relations, productivity, self-realization, and the like. Available measuring instruments, like tests and rating scales, are for the most part inadequate for this kind of assessment. Does it follow that the changes desired by dynamic therapists do not occur? I do not think so. What seems to follow is that our measuring instruments are insufficiently sensitive.

Of course, it is possible that if we had fully adequate tools, the alleged personality changes might be shown to occur infrequently or sporadically, which would be a more serious indictment, but even if this were true a therapist and a patient might still want to take the risk, either because this form of psychotherapy appeals to them as an educational process, because other forms of therapy do not seem any more promising, or for other reasons. This does not mean that therapists subscribing to diverse orientations could not agree on certain rules or criteria, but as long as such common ground has not been established one cannot conclude that a given technique or outcome is superior on scientific grounds.

The dynamically oriented therapist would contend

that there are valid reasons for a person's reluctance to speak in public, which manifest themselves as an inhibition. If he goes against this inhibition or is forced to do so by the requirements of a college course, he may experience anxiety, which is also reflected in physiological and autonomic indices. He wants to master the course, he is concerned about the instructor's and fellow students' approval, but something within him says no. Subjectively, he feels "I can't," which could also mean "I don't want to." In short, he is in conflict. Now contrast the approach of the behavior therapist with that of the dynamic therapist.

The behavior therapist is not interested in "underlying reasons;" he will assert that at some time in the past the anxiety response has become conditioned to a previously neutral stimulus. But this is not essential for the therapy. His approach basically is to counter-condition the anxiety response. The therapist achieves this by asking the patient to imagine anxiety-provoking situations in a graduated series and by teaching him to make responses antagonistic to anxiety, notably relaxation, whereupon the anxiety response is gradually diminished. Having in this way achieved mastery over his anxiety, the therapeutic gain may radiate to other areas of the patient's living.

The dynamic therapist, on the other hand, views the anxiety response as a possible manifestation of more general personality dispositions, such as avoidance of challenging situations and dependence (Andrews, 1966). If this hypothesis is correct, he may find there are numerous situations, besides public speaking, in which the patient experiences anxiety, shrinks from challenges, and fails to assert himself. He may gradually isolate a common theme linking these experiences, which he will bring to the patient's attention as the evidence accumulates. Throughout, he will enlist the patient's cooperation in verbalizing his associations, fantasies, etc. As the therapeutic work proceeds, it may develop that the patient is fiercely competitive with his peers (to whom he may react as younger siblings) or he may fantasy that whenever he asserts himself (as in public speaking) he is in danger of expressing rage toward an authority figure who may retaliate, with dire consequences. He gains insight into his feelings and behavior by experiencing the affect in relation to the therapist, who interprets the patient's current feelings in terms of his past experience and demonstrates to him how seemingly diverse situations are interrelated and the manner in which he misconstrues the present in terms of the past. Clearly, this work requires time and cannot be accomplished in five hours. It proceeds on the general hypothesis that as implicit processes are made explicit, and as the patient struggles with his difficulties, he will achieve greater control and mastery.

Is this tedious excursion necessary? Is it worth the trouble? The answer obviously depends upon the circumstances. If the patient is greatly disturbed by his phobic fears, if clinical assessments show that the public-speaking anxiety is an instance of a more pervasive disturbance, if the patient is interested in gaining an understanding of his feelings and motives instead of merely being relieved of his symptoms, and if other conditions are met, the answer may be in the affirmative. In the case of Paul's subjects, none of whom apparently saw the need for psychotherapy until they were solicited, and for whom the fear of public speaking seemed to be an isolated symptom of minimal severity, there clearly was no need.

"Insight therapy" is not designed for the purpose intended by Paul, and it seems absurd to restrict therapists following some semblance of the approach sketched above to five hours, to see how much "insight" the patient can acquire and to what extent the symptom might yield.

What Paul's study has shown is that, given the circumstances he contrived, desensitization appears to work quite well, and numerous other studies support his findings. He is entitled to conclude that under the stated conditions (and presumably similar ones) this form of psychotherapy—for which he personally shows a preference—is helpful. What he has failed to do, as I have attempted to show, is (1) to study dynamic psychotherapy as it is commonly practiced, instead of which he devised a form of brief psychotherapy arbitrarily defined as "insight therapy;" and (2) to demonstrate the superiority of therapies based on a learning model to those based on dynamic conceptions. In my judgment Paul's generalizations are not justified, largely because the comparisons he made are not the proper ones to make. If Paul's findings are restricted to the conditions of his experiment they may be accepted as such. One should be extremely wary, however, of generalizing the conclusions, as Paul and others citing his work have done. For the indicated reasons, there are as yet no adequate comparisons of the type intended by Paul. Consequently, there is no reliable evidence for the superiority of one therapeutic approach over another, and even less of the effectiveness of psychotherapy compared to no treatment.

An Example of Retrospective Outcome Research

The research whose salient findings I propose to summarize in the following was based on two investigations (Strupp, Wallach, and Wogan, 1964; Strupp, Fox, and Lessler, 1969) which were prominently concerned with former patients' retrospective accounts of their psychotherapy experience. Briefly, we obtained extensive questionnaire data from two samples of former patients (a sample of 44 patients seen by private practitioners for a mean of 166 interviews, and a second, larger sample of 122 clinic patients who for the most part were seen by psychiatric residents for a mean of 70 interviews). These were bona fide patients and the severity of their difficulties was evidenced by the fact that about one-third had previously been hospitalized for psychiatric reasons. All underwent either psychoanalysis or psychoanalytically oriented psychotherapy. The subjective data supplied by the patients were complemented by ratings from their therapists and data abstracted from clinic charts.

Unlike Paul's study, this was not an experimental

investigation in which the form of psychotherapy was manipulated, nor was it possible to exercise control over many other variables. The principal merit of this research, in our judgment, derived from the patients' own observations, comments, and evaluations, the comparisons with objective data we were able to perform, and the extent to which the patients' assertions about their therapy experience dovetailed with observations typically made by clinicians and also found in the clinical literature.

On the basis of several indices we concluded that two-thirds to three-quarters of the patients participating in our surveys considered their therapy experience valuable; they reported that they had greatly benefited from it; and they attributed significant changes in personality and behavior to their psychotherapy. What was the nature of these changes?

Most noteworthy, perhaps, was the relatively minor emphasis they assigned to improvements of the common neurotic symptoms, such as anxiety, depression, and physical disturbances. This contrasted sharply with the more impressive changes (at least in terms of frequency of mention) in the areas of interpersonal relations and self-esteem. The conclusion emerged that the patients' view of therapeutic changes merged with that of all analytically oriented therapists. That is, therapeutic changes were seen not in terms of "symptom removal" but as changes occurring on a broader front and affecting the broad spectrum of their life experience. Since our respondents did not speak as clinicians but as laymen, we should put the matter more precisely by stating that these changes were most salient in the patients' awareness and were valued most highly. These findings argue against a conception of analytic psychotherapy as a technique for the "removal" of specific symptoms; instead they highlight more general character and personality changes. Patients frequently reported a new orientation toward life in general, a modified outlook on reality, and changes in their self-concept. Related findings pertained to the patients' assertion that changes were apparent to close associates, and that they had occurred relatively rapidly once therapy got under way.

One of the trenchant accomplishments of psychotherapy with this population (as probably with most patients) was the transformation of seemingly mysterious and mystifying symptoms into phenomena which had explainable antecedents. Following therapy, the causes of the patient's difficulties were viewed in the context of his interpersonal relations. At the same time, this new understanding was accompanied by the development of techniques for more adaptive, less conflictual, and more satisfying ways of relating to others. An integral part of this learning experience undoubtedly was the achievement of a sense of mastery over experiences that hitherto had appeared as events to be passively endured. Conceptualizations of such therapeutic changes may, of course, be found in the writings of a host of therapists—from Freud to Erikson—but they have seldom been documented by reports of patients who had undergone psychotherapy. As Fromm-Reichmann (1950) stated:

In going over the literature on anxiety in children and adults, from M. Klein, Sharpe and Spitz, to Ferenczi and Rank, Freud, Rado, and Sullivan, Fromm, Horney and Silverberg, it seems that the feelings of powerlessness, of helplessness in the presence of inner dangers, which the individual cannot control, constitute in the last analysis the common background of all further elaborations on the theory of anxiety.

It was precisely these feelings of helplessness and inability to cope which were ubiquitous both in the presenting complaints and in the areas of improvement listed by our patients. Gradually, in the course of therapy, feelings of self-confidence, self-assurance, and mastery replaced self-perceptions of helplessness, inadequacy, and overwhelming despair. Or, stated in different terms, the natural tendencies toward synthesis, meaning, organization, competence, and growth supplanted the patient's previous sense of failure and helplessness.

No single variable emerged as highly predictive of therapeutic outcome and, in view of the complexity of the factors and their interacting effects, such a result was hardly to be expected. Patients, however, who met certain criteria appeared more assured of success than those who did not share these factors: (1) somewhat older, married patients, with children; (2) relatively recent onset of disturbance; (3) greater adherence to scheduled interviews; (4) greater internal pressure at the beginning of therapy; (5) relatively rapid improvement once therapy got under way; (6) less incapacitation, as judged by the clinic; and (7) greater motivation for psychotherapy, as judged by the clinic.

Finally, the therapist's attitudes toward the patient, the quality of their working relationhip, and the patient's feeling of being respected by the therapist were shown to be important in determining the final outcome. In contrast, length of therapy, frequency of sessions, and intensity of the emotional experience as perceived by the patient had no demonstrable bearing on outcome.

In the absence of comprehensive data on the patient-therapist interaction, specific information about the techniques employed, and because of gaps in our knowledge of the nature of therapy in general, we do not as yet know how personality and behavior changes are achieved. Our work, however, provided some important clues. The typical psychotherapy experience we examined was neither superficial nor very intensive (in the sense of attempting radical personality change). It helped the patient work through certain traumatic experiences; it succeeded in clarifying some patterns of neurotic interaction; and, above all, it provided a corrective emotional experience (Alexander and French, 1946).

The latter is perhaps the most important and central point of the therapeutic encounter we have studied; judging from their reports, patients experienced a hitherto unknown degree of acceptance, understanding, and respect; and within the framework of benevolent neutrality and warmth they were encouraged to examine some of the more troublesome aspects of their behavior and attitudes.

Certainly, the therapeutic experience provided a sharp contrast to other human relationships the patients had previously known; it was an antidote to the criticism, exploitation, and dependency that they had encouraged themselves or of which they had been the victim; it permitted freedom to experience shameful, anxiety-provoking, and other painful feelings, and it supplied the patients with a professional helper who insisted that they look at themselves, examine some of the problems in their lives and work out—on an emotional as well as a cognitive level—a more viable solution. There is little question that this approach resulted in increased self-acceptance, self-respect, and competence.

Therapists generally employed psychoanalytic principles (in a broad sense) rather than persuasion, suggestion, and the like. No matter how faltering and imperfect the procedure, the data demonstrated that they worked. Were the results due to suggestion? Did the patients become converts to a new faith? We cannot prove or disprove either possibility, but whatever their nature the results in many instances were impressive and lasting. There is also reason to believe that they were achieved by rational means, that is, by procedures which at least in principle are teachable, communicable, and replicable. Could more have been achieved within the available time, by greater experts, by more incisive techniques? Perhaps. But something tangible was achieved, and it represented partly a measurable, partly a more elusive social and personal gain to the recipients.

The skeptic who insists on seeing the presenting symptom as the problem and denies the importance of intrapsychic conflicts and underlying causes will, of course, not be convinced by these demonstrations. He will counter that the patients' reports may merely reflect the therapist's success in persuading the patient or in instilling a new faith in the authority of the healer. True, we do not know what the patients' retrospective accounts would have been like had they been treated by therapists following a different theoretical orientation, but there can be little doubt that for these particular patients, treated by analytically oriented psychotherapy, a shift in outlook and orientation occurred and that it took these particular forms.

It is probably true that most of our patients were reasonably mature, as shown by their ability to function in the community despite their neurotic handicaps. However, it is equally important to note that they often suffered from chronic and severe difficulties in living. The data showed that in an appreciable number of cases even such problems were helped markedly by psychotherapy of the kind studied by us. They also strengthened our conviction, which appears to be insufficiently appreciated by behavioristic psychology, that in effective psychotherapy the patient achieves subjective gains which defy quantification. Such gains include interpersonal competence, mastery, and concomitant increments in self-esteem.

Finally, it is important to draw attention to the

uniqueness of the psychotherapeutic situation as a vehicle for personal growth and maturation. There are many elements which the psychotherapeutic relationship shares with other interpersonal experiences, characterized by openness, acceptance, and understanding. Such resemblance, however, does not signify identity.

Qualities which set the psychotherapeutic situation apart from other human encounters include the therapist's objectivity, his sharply circumscribed involvement in the patient's life, his training which enables him to detect neurotic entanglements and self-defeating maneuvers, and his commitment to help the patient arrive at his own solutions by the process of examining and understanding factors within himself which contribute to his difficulties in living.

At its best, individual psychotherapy creates conditions for such learning unequaled by anything human ingenuity has been able to devise, and it represents a powerful affirmation of the individual's worth, self-direction, and independence. While costly in terms of money, time, manpower, and dedication of the participants to the common task, it remains one of the few oases in a collectivistic society that in a host of ways fosters conformity and erodes individual values and autonomy. From a practical standpoint, it cannot begin to cope effectively with the enormity of human suffering caused by destructive interpersonal experience, and no amount of refinement in technique can significantly increase its effectiveness to a point where it could be considered a widely applicable weapon in man's armamentarium against neurotic problems. In essence, it remains an unrealizable ideal of self-discovery through learning and teaching in the context of a human relationship uninfluenced by ulterior motives of indoctrination or social control. What the patient, if he is fortunate, may expect is a glimpse or even a reasonable approximation.

On the basis of all our evidence we concluded that outpatient psychotherapy, as it is commonly practiced in this country, performs a highly useful function and that patients who meet certain criteria and have the good fortune to find a competent therapist may expect to benefit substantially. At the same time, we found little evidence to support the view that clinics operate at a high level of efficiency or that they offer a great deal to a sizable segment of the individuals who apply for help.

The two kinds of studies I have briefly reviewed obviously represent very different approaches to research in psychotherapy, but they share the view that (1) the effectiveness of psychotherapy is a legitimate area for scientific inquiry; and (2) there must be a continuing search for methods which meet more effectively and more efficiently the enormous social needs for psychotherapeutic services. If "traditional" psychotherapy lived up to these requirements, obviously there would be no pressure to search for new techniques. Unfortunately, we are confronted with a growing hiatus between supply and demand (i.e., between the services offered and the patient's real or imagined needs), and it is this gap which will somehow be filled. As concerned people, scientists, and professionals it is our responsibility to ensure that the new approaches are sound, sophisticated, and efficient as well as humane.

CONCLUSIONS

In conclusion, because psychotherapy has traditionally been regarded as a variant of medical treatment, terms like "cure," "improvement," and so on have been employed as seemingly reasonable criteria. They are not. As I have tried to indicate, the issue is still befogged. It is safe to predict that clarification of the criterion problem, that is, the kinds of changes that may be expected from particular psychotherapeutic procedures, will be clarified to the extent that the medical analogizing will be abandoned. Paradoxically, psychologists who have pioneered psychotherapeutic techniques anchored to learning theory principles have continued to measure the efficacy of their endeavors along similar "mental health" lines.

It would help greatly to view psychotherapy as a form of education, or, as Freud called it, an "after-education." What the patient in psychotherapy acquires is new perceptions of himself and others; he learns new patterns of interpersonal behavior but he also has to unlearn maladaptive, old ones. There are vast individual differences in the capacity to profit from different kinds of learning situations just as there are such differences in the educational realm. Psychoanalysis, as one form of psychotherapy, may be likened to a form of graduate education, and like graduate education it is suitable for only relatively few comers. As long as the patient's suitability for a given form of therapy is decided on factual or clinical grounds, rather than in terms of his ability to pay for necessarily expensive services, there can be no quarrel. To be sure, some deserving students are excluded from advanced university training because they lack financial resources, but society is aware of the problem and attempts to remedy it through scholarships and the like. The same considerations should apply to prospective candidates for psychoanalysis or psychotherapy. Szasz (1965) put it this way:

The evidence suggests that, when the various forms of psychotherapy are clearly identified, each will appeal to and hence be useful for only certain kinds of *persons.* I am confident that this will be true, not only for psychoanalysis, but for other forms of psychotherapy as well. The scope of a particular psychotherapeutic method is limited, not so much by the nature of the client's "mental disease" as it is by his education, interests, and values. Different *people,* not different mental *diseases,* require differing psychiatric methods. Since psychotherapists cannot adjust their methods to the "needs" of their clients, the only rational solution lies in clearly identifying therapists. Clients will then be able to find therapists whose methods are compatible with their own interests and standards (page 43).

Research can play an important role, it seems to me, in identifying which particular methods of psychotherapy are suitable for which particular people. Once a therapist works toward realistic goals with a given individual we shall be able to abandon futile attempts to determine which therapeutic method is "most effective." For some persons a form of "behavior modification" may be the best that can be hoped for; for others the achievement of greater autonomy through self-discovery in psychoanalysis may be the goal. Within each category, there will be slow and fast "learners." In each instance, the method must be tailored to the individual, which is the reason general principles of psychotherapy can provide only the grossest guidelines. Different teachers (or therapists) also have their individual styles, and some can work more productively with some students (or patients) than with others. Each therapist-teacher, despite thorough training, is bound to make his share of mistakes, which suggests that patient effort, hard work, an inquiring attitude, and, above all, a sense of humility are the only sensible approach to psychotherapy.

REFERENCES

ALEXANDER F., and T. M. FRENCH. *Psychoanalytic Therapy: Principles and Applications.* New York: Ronald Press, 1946.

ANDREWS, J. D. W. Psychotherapy of phobias. *Psychological Bulletin,* 1966, **66**:455–480.

COLBY, K. M. Psychotherapeutic processes. *Annual Review of Psychology,* 1964, **15**:347–370.

EYSENCK, H. J. The effects of psychotherapy: An evaluation. *Journal of Consulting Psychology,* 1952, **16**:319–324.

EYSENCK, H. J. The effects of psychotherapy, in H. J. Eysenck (ed.), *Handbook of Abnormal Psychology.* New York: Basic Books, 1961.

FROMM-REICHMANN, F. *Principles of Intensive Psychotherapy.* Chicago: University of Chicago Press, 1950.

KNIGHT, K. P. Evaluation of the results of psychoanalytic therapy. *Amer. J. Psychiat.,* 1941, **98**:434–446.

MATARAZZO, J. D. Psychotherapeutic processes. *Annual Review of Psychology,* 1965, **16**:181–224.

PAUL, G. L. *Insight vs. Desensitization in Psychotherapy.* Stanford: Stanford University Press, 1966.

STRUPP, H. H. Psychotherapy revisited: The problem of outcome. *Psychotherapy,* 1963, **1**:1–13.

STRUPP, H. H. Psychoanalytic therapy of the individual, in J. Marmor (ed.), *Modern Psychoanalysis.* New York: Basic Books, 1968. Pp. 293–342.

STRUPP, H. H., R. E. FOX, and K. LESSLER. *Patients View Their Psychotherapy.* Baltimore: The Johns Hopkins Press, 1969.

STRUPP, H. H., M. S. WALLACH, and M. WOGAN. Psychotherapy experience in retrospect: A questionnaire survey of former patients and their therapists. *Psychological Monographs,* 1964, 78 (Whole No. 588).

SZASZ, T. S. *The Ethics of Psychoanalysis.* New York: Basic Books, 1965.

SZASZ, T. S. Behavior therapy and psychoanalysis. *Medical Opinion and Review,* 1967 (June), 24–29.

WOLMAN, B. B. Evidence in psychoanalytic research. *Journ. Amer. Psychoanal. Assn,* 1964, **12**:717–733.

WOLPE, J. *Psychotherapy by Reciprocal Inhibition.* Stanford: Stanford University Press, 1958.

PART THREE
Clinical Experiences

Some Problems in Psychoanalytic Technique

LEON J. SAUL, M.D.

THE GOALS TREATMENT

THE GOAL of treatment of mental disorders is the correction of pathodynamics, which consists primarily of disordered emotional patterns of reactions to other persons formed especially before about age six. The earlier they are formed and the more deep-seated they are the more difficult they are to influence by any form of psychological therapy available to us today. Only the emotional problems encountered in ordinary office practice are considered here and do not include the psychoses or conditions primarily reactive to traumatic situations such as war or, of course, organic brain disorders.

The model here is of an individual born with certain developmental trends—trends conditioned by the treatment he received from those responsible for and close to him as a child, especially during his earliest years, thereby shaping a pattern of emotional attitudes, feelings, and reactions toward other human beings. This emotional pattern continues within his personality for life, as he interacts in his culture and in his personal psychological field, which in part he makes for himself and which in part is imposed upon him. Stated succinctly, each individual interacts with other persons with his innate drives toward development and adaptation and his persisting childhood patterns, both of which have been conditioned most powerfully during his earliest years but also by later experiences.

If the individual comes to us for therapy because of great conflict or tension with his environment, this may be primarily because of the stresses of his current environment to which no one, however stable and flexible, could adapt; it might be from failure of his particular personality to fit the particular field; it may be a failure in his own capacity for adaptation; and at the extreme, the problem may arise primarily because of conflict, failures, or warpings of development within the individual himself which cause difficulties no matter what the environment. These disorders of development we find regularly to stem from pathological emotional problems formed during the earliest years, especially until about six years of age, by the treatment the person experienced as a child at the hands of others.

If our conceptual model is correct, then it becomes clear that in the predominantly internal problems arising chiefly from within the personality the task of causal therapy is to correct the pathological emotional patterns formed in childhood. Since these patterns consist of feelings toward other persons, they can be adequately corrected only by working them through as feelings toward one or more other persons. It was one of Freud's great discoveries that patients transfer these patterns to others, including the analyst. Thus the relationship to the analyst is in effect a sample human relationship. The disordered childhood pattern repeats itself in some part and form to the therapist. The task is to work with the mature part of the patient's personality in shared responsibilities, analyzing out the pathological elements, thereby releasing the patient's potential for continuing his natural emotional development.

Freud frequently compared analytic therapy with surgery. In his *Outline of Psychoanalysis,* he calls it "after-education." It has similarities to both. For example, a young girl is much criticized and restricted by her mother. The reaction she develops is rebellious hostility to the mother expressed in behavior meant to defy her. This behavior is in danger of bringing the child to the attention of the police and also of having her expelled from school, damaging her reputation. The surgery in this case consists of a "hostilotomy." If the analyst can make conscious, work through, show other ways of reacting and by all other methods available to him reduce the girl's hostility to her mother so that she can handle this relationship without the defiant, hostile, self-punitive acting out, then the danger is reduced—like lowering the basal metabolism by removing part of the thyroid to reduce its secretions. Of course, this involves also helping the girl understand the other major emotional forces, specifically the mother's domination and criticism, and the girl's self-defense against this by hostile rebellion. This opens up other ways of dealing with her mother which are less injurious to both and are more consonant with good relations and with the forces of maturing. If the defense is no longer needed, or is replaced by other, more mature reactions, then the hostility and the consequent masochistic, self-injurious behavior are undercut. This is a sort of psychological surgery.

At the same time, as after-education, the analyst comes to stand during treatment, just as Freud said, in the place of a parent and can provide the insights and the attitudes of sympathetic understanding freed of those other attitudes of the mother which cause the girl's hostile reaction to her. Thus also—as Freud described—the analyst, through the patient's projecting her superego onto him, is in a position to correct the "parental blunder." The patient learns to distinguish between her childhood reactions to a parent and her present-day reactions as an adult to the analyst who is not her parent.

The degree of success achieved by the analyst, regardless of his method and technique depends upon the balance of forces in the patient and his or her fixity. How influenceable they are is determined by such factors as the intensity and degree of the forces; how early in the child's life they were exerted; how frequent, consistent and unrelieved they were; how long they continued; what balancing and compensating factors there are; and similar variables.

Apart from the balance of forces within the patient, therapeutic progress also depends on the skill and personality of the analyst and thus upon how well suited the analyst is to the particular personality and problems of the patient. There is disagreement on this point, and some analysts still believe that any analyst can treat any person with equal effectiveness. This is no place to advance empirical data, and I will state only that the conclusion from my three decades of experience is that the choice of analyst for a particular patient is of great importance in many cases. This is in part because the therapeutic results, about the dynamics of which in an individual case we have a great deal to learn, depend not only upon the depth and accuracy of the analyst's understanding and interpretations but also upon the successful transference to the analyst of the neurotic patient's disturbed childhood motivations and their derivatives. How these develop, the ways in which the analyst deals with them, his feelings about them, and his feelings about the patient are all indicative of the analyst's personality as well as of his insight and skills. His personality creates an emotional climate in which the whole treatment is conducted.

Reduced to simplest terms, as Freud said, "the patient puts the analyst in the place of his father (or mother)" thereby "giving him the power which his superego exercises over his ego." Thus the analyst's personality becomes an inevitable part of the patient's new superego. Insight alone on the part of the analyst is insufficient; equally inadequate, sometimes even dangerous, is a supportive attitude without insight (Saul, 1958). For example, a girl felt guilt because of a sexual transgression and remained depressed despite kindly reassurance from her therapist. She only improved when given insight into the sources of her exaggerated guilt in the extreme puritanism of her father. Conversely, a young man felt that there were certain things he simply could never tell the analyst. The young man knew this was a pattern he had had toward his mother. This insight alone did not help. He had to have the experience of testing the analyst, telling these things bit by bit, cautiously feeling his way to prove the truth of his own insight; he had to discriminate between his conditioning by a threatening mother and the present reality of full freedom to reveal himself to the analyst with the prospect of approval instead of punishment from a shocked parent.

Insofar as the analyst provides the attitudes of tolerance, sympathy, and understanding, free from traumatic elements, coupled with insight into the patient's emotional pattern, its development, history, and the way in which it operates, he is imparting insight and understanding in a fashion which justifies calling it "after-education." The procedure opens the patient's mind to much that is going on in his reactions as well as in the reactions of others. In the deepening and broadening of the patient's understanding, his mind is freed from some of the automatic patterns of reaction formed in childhood and used reflexively in adulthood.

The patient sees the possibility of new ways of reacting; for example, the girl mentioned previously, with the overly critical, restrictive, controlling mother, can learn to handle the relationship to her mother in ways other than by hostile, self-injurious acting out. New choices are opened up, which also increases adaptability and flexibility. Put another way, the girl is desensitized in some degree to her mother's constant interfering efforts at frustrating control so that the girl does not pain her mother and damage herself in her rebellious reactions to this.

Insofar as the relationship is better understood and better handled, it no longer absorbs so much of the patient's energy. Therefore it increases the free energy and, with the decrease of tension, also increases the capacity for relaxation. The patient has been conditioned to react in a certain way, and the analytic therapeutic procedure is intelligible as a method of deconditioning and reconditioning. The patient no longer need have his life lived for him from within because of the aftereffects of the treatment he received during childhood—the way he was conditioned then, or, in psychoanalytic terms, the internalization of the parental figures and the continued reactions to these introjects as his superego. He becomes increasingly able to live his life through the judgment of his ego rather than the automaticity of his superego, which in turn increases his capacity to learn from experience.

Since the problem is primarily a continuation of faulty human relationships, its correction also results in improved relations with other persons. With the growth of his judgment and understanding his sense of reality improves, and he is less dominated by views of others and of himself which were imposed by the treatment he received from those responsible for him and by his interplay of feelings with them. He can see himself less as a small child and more realistically appraise his capacity as a grown adult with personality, intelligence, and physical powers for responsibility and productivity. A more realistic view of himself, a healthier self-image, or, what is similar, a mature ego identity can make an enormous difference to the patient in living his life. This is in part because the way people respond to us is determined so largely not only by how we feel toward them but by how we feel toward ourselves. With the reduction of the pathological emotional patterns, inner frustration is reduced and capacities are increased for satisfaction in real life.

Mental and emotional health is largely, in simple terms, a matter of maturity combined with adjustment. There are situations, as the war showed us, in which it is easier for a childish, egocentric personality to adjust, thinking only of himself, without much sense of responsibility for others, than it is for a mature person with a developed sense of responsibility and reality and capacity to love, who has on his mind the welfare of the men in his command and of his wife and children at home.

Our overall goal is to release the patient's emotional development out of the automatic pathological emotional pattern so that he can mature to his full capacity to enjoy loving and being loved, working and playing —a balanced, mature life insofar as it is possible in the world today. Put another way, a major goal of treatment is to turn the patient from fixations in certain responses—to turn him, through reopening the development, from being on the way in to movement on the way out.

Needless to say, these goals are not achieved in the office alone. Here the patient has the total analytic experience, the emotional experience of transference and countertransference, the insights and working through, and everything that he can learn from the analyst. But a vital part of the goal consists in helping the patient make use of this experience in his living. This, like his symptom, is a matter of the balance of forces within the patient. It is determined by all those influences upon him, especially during earliest childhood, which permitted him to develop properly and gave him his strengths. Finally, it is only practice in living, the patient's capacity to use the analytic experience, which will further him on his way to these goals. That, too, insofar as possible, the analyst must help him with, perhaps by what he does not do as much as by what he does.

Broadening the Scope of Treatment

A woman came to see me because of a marital problem which had made her lose both respect and sexual interest in her husband, whereas the husband was made to feel immature, inadequate, and inferior. In our discussion of the progress made in the husband's analysis I was told of the husband's infantile erotisms, which his analyst believed had nothing to do with the wife but was purely the husband's internal matter. Although the husband's analyst was aware of the dynamics and their genesis in how the patient was treated in childhood, he simply ignored this etiology in the patient's life and in therapy. He noted the husband's dependence, but considered this to be chiefly oral erotism unrelated to the wife and the marital disharmony. The unconscious hostility, which undercurrent was so important in the patient's masochism and in the marital friction, was noted but not dealt with, nor were the patient's feelings of inferiority—perhaps because Freud never wrote about these except by implication, as part of the castration complex.

"Cruel and sadistic tendencies find satisfaction in this dream," wrote Freud of Dora in "Fragment of an Analysis of a Case of Hysteria," when he published her case as an example of the psychosexual etiology of hysteria. Freud used the term "psychosexual" to take cognizance of more than sensuality alone. He could not explore and illumine everything. Perhaps in the case of little Hans, Freud did not give due weight to tensions between the parents which led to divorce as a factor which created anxiety and resentment in the child and thereby influenced his sensual fantasies. But today we are not lone explorers of a tangled unknown: Freud showed the way and decades have passed.

The two patients just mentioned were not classic examples of hysteria, nor were they classic examples of neurosis in the restricted sense of showing anxiety, conversion, phobia, or compulsion. Yet both had been treated psychoanalytically as if their problems were based exclusively on sexual etiology.

Indeed, although some analysts of highest standing still distinguish sharply between neuroses and personality disorders, clinical facts do not support this distinction, nor is the distinction consistent with psychoanalytic theory of the personality structure and psychopathology. The emotional forces which form the infantile motivational pattern in both its healthy and disturbed aspects find expression in many ways of thinking, feeling, and behaving, however wholesome the ego. The health, strength, and nature of an individual's ego are themselves results of influences upon the individual during his earliest years. This pattern of emotional forces is the essential. In neuroses, the superego never is entirely mature and healthy because of its very nature—being the internalized pattern of treatment and identifications during early childhood, including those which formed the infantile neurosis, foundation of the neurosis in the adult. If treatment of the child and parental models of feelings, attitude, and behavior all were proper for health, growth, and development, basically good personal relations and relative freedom from emotional problems would be the rule in the adult.

Moreover, modern knowledge of the ego concludes that, in Freud's words: "Neuroses are, as we know, disorders of the ego." We all have almost every impulse; adjustment depends largely on how we handle them. Thus today neurosis is conceived of as combining effects of disordered id, superego, and ego.

Id, ego, and superego comprise the total personality. Disorders in these structures are by definition disorders of personality. Disorders of ego and superego are bound to permeate the total personality, which they affect in many ways. The modern concept of neurosis as a disorder involving ego and superego obliterates the distinction between neurosis and personality disorders, and neurosis becomes one particular form of personality disorder. The personality disorder is primary; the specific nature of the symptoms—whether neurosis, perversion, behavior disorder, or whatever—is secondary, resulting from the specific balance (or rather, imbalance) of forces.

Sensual behavior of the child is one factor which can disturb the emotional interrelations with the parents; this is internalized, as Freud has described, and makes the psychopathology, involving id, ego, and superego in varying degrees. Infantile sexuality can be disordered by excessive prohibitions and threats, and by seductions such as kissing too fervently on the lips, too much fondling, stimulation of the anal region or the genitals, and so on. Very often the disturbed sexuality is a consequence of disturbed feelings, motivations, and reactions—disordered by poor child-rearing, with poor personal emotional relationships. In turn, these disturbed relations derange many other functions and areas of the personality. Sexuality is one area that suffers. The key lies in feelings generated in the child toward emotionally important persons. The early conditioning persists in some degree for life. Because child-rearing is generally so atrocious, most personalities are considerably warped and the world is the neurotic, criminal place we know, with a variety of disorders produced by an equal variety of abuses in child-rearing.

No analyst helps every patient; some patients even get worse, as is the case throughout medical practice. But there are legitimate and illegitimate failures. If the patient has had the best possible treatment within the present state of our knowledge, we feel that everything possible has been done. But when one is consulted by a series of patients whose basic dynamics either were not understood or dealt with—all of whom were treated psychoanalytically as though they had had a single circumscribed hysterical symptom with a presumedly exclusively infantile sexual etiology—then it becomes an obligation to report the matter for discussion.

The libido theory alone is not an adequate scientific conceptual model for comprehending the realities of an individual patient's psychopathology and for helping to correct this. Freud's later interpersonal model, psychoanalysis as after-education to correct parental blunders incorporated as superego, is effective.

Psychoanalysis is a powerful instrument: If the rationale is not mastered and the realities of the patient's motivations and reactions not clearly comprehended, the power of psychoanalytic treatment may harm rather than help.

I should like to speak of a series of cases in which the patients were seen after they had had between 600 and 900 hours of classical psychoanalytic treatment— mostly five days per week on the couch—conducted by a number of experienced analysts. The patients showed striking similarities in their complaints: Each was depressed and anxious, with a sense of failure and a frightening loss of self-confidence. In each instance the patient was almost impossible to live with at home or work, was deeply embittered, and felt his self-control threatened. Each wished bitterly that he was as he had been prior to treatment.

Although these individuals had been treated by different analysts, they had in common the following:

1. The infantile libidinal impulses had been analyzed with little reference to the patient's emotional problems or to the causes of impairment in the patient's development; in other words, sensuality had been concentrated upon at the expense of feelings, emotional patterns toward self and others, and the total personality. Deficiency of efforts to correct aftereffects of traumatic influences or parental "blunders" resembled treating a fever without dealing with its underlying cause.

2. Concentration of the analyst upon the infantile libidinal impulses without relation to the patient's current real emotional problems made the patient feel criticized, deprecated, and inferior.

3. As the analyst became dissatisfied and irritated by the worsening of the patient's condition, the analyst's feelings gradually crept into the countertransference and, as time passed, the patient incorporated the analyst's critical attitudes into a new depreciatory, critical superego rather than the correcting, supporting, and understanding superego necessary for the patient.

4. Inevitably (as Freud described), the analyst stood in the place of the parent in the patient's mind, but the analyst did not use this transference for after-education and correction. However thoroughly the sexuality was analyzed, the interrelationship and interplay of

the feelings between child and parent (or "substitute" parent) either was neglected, misunderstood, or ignored in treating the patient. This quintessential of psychoanalytic treatment—not sensual impulses alone, but the major emotional forces, the childhood pattern of psychodynamics toward the parents in relation to the patient's current real life and to the transference —this fundamental was missed.

This is the critical point, I believe, in the status of psychoanalysis today and for its future development: the central importance of the persisting pathodynamic emotional pattern formed in early childhood in reaction to how the child was treated by those responsible for it and closest to it.

5. The patient's reactions to the analyst's countertransference feelings of dissatisfaction were not analyzed; therefore, they became stronger and deeper, the patient feeling more and more ashamed, guilty, unwanted, and inadequate—a failure in the eyes of this newly developing superego. Theoretically the analyst should have no such countertransference reaction, but a physician cannot watch a patient make major sacrifices in time, money, and emotion and remain unmoved as, over months and years, the patient's condition worsens.

6. Rather than being reduced by accurate, realistic analysis of its origins, the hostility from the patient's own emotional pattern was augmented by inadequate analysis, by the frustrations of the analysis, and by the countertransference. This hostility built up to a degree which taxed the patient's capacity to handle it, causing

severe emotional tension, strain, anxiety, insomnia, psychosomatic symptoms, depression, fear of breakdown, hostile behavior, and guilt. In one case the hostility was so overt that the patient almost lost his wife and his position; the analyst had permitted "expression" of hostility in the transference, but the unconscious sources of the hostility in transference-repetition of the childhood pattern were not analyzed, whereupon the hostility was mobilized but not reduced, and it became impossible to live with the patient.

7. Long periods during which the analyst remained silent when the patient was upset and confused, enraged the patient and increased his turmoil, guilt, and shame. Usually the patient understood the silence in terms of his own increasingly critical superego, i.e., as lack of interest, rejection, criticism, and censure.

These persons did not come to treatment with severe emotional illnesses. The rationale behind their treatment reveals a systematic error. No doubt all good analysts recognize the main dynamics, i.e., the childhood pattern of feelings toward family members formed by attitudes and behavior in the rearing of the child, and inappropriately continuing in the adult; but apparently these emotional forces are not always clearly, directly, goal-consciously analyzed in actual therapy—chiefly because the emphasis on a too exclusively sexual theory of personality and of the etiology of the neuroses distorts perception of these other forces. Because of this persisting historical bias, other forces and relationships are perceived but not appreciated or effectively used in treatment.

THE SENSE OF IDENTITY

Historically, the development of psychoanalysis has depended very largely on the achievement of insight; first into the nature of neurotic symptoms and then into the nature of the personality, including the relationship with self and with others. To judge by the literature, emphasis in treatment is naturally upon the achievement of insight. When this is difficult, because of resistances, then the procedure is to obtain insight into the nature of the resistances. It is generally recognized that insight alone does not cure the patient's difficulties. Another important and well-recognized element is the transference—the relationship of the patient to the therapist. The handling of this, however, also involves insight; that is, the gradual discerning of how the patient repeats with the analyst his old relationships and conflicts with persons in childhood. The patient obtains support from the transference relationship; this is inadequate without insight and even somewhat risky, since it makes the patient too dependent on the analyst.

If insight into the transference relationship alone does not resolve the patient's problem, what does? The usual answer is "working through," which, however, is largely a matter of more insight into the patient's emotional patterns as they are repeated in different aspects and facets of the transference and of his life.

Is there not more that can be done to make use of the insight for which we strive? It has been recognized that the patient's absorption in his conflict makes him see life as holding a limited number of choices. For example, a young man who has had a very domineering mother may feel that there are only two attitudes: to be submissive, as he was to her, or to domineer by way of an identification with her. Locked in this relationship, he sees only the two roles, the child's toward the mother or the mother's toward the child. In such a situation it must indeed be legitimate for the analyst to point out the unreality of the patient's thinking and to discuss with him solutions to the conflict.

How, then, do we make the most effective therapeutic use of the insight which we obtain? Certainly many analysts, while agreeing with what we have said here, in actual practice appear only to keep repeating the same interpretations, and if the patient does not progress to recommend "more analysis," perhaps with a different analyst. Often, however, the process of making the unconscious conscious goes on for long periods of time without improvement in the patient. In fact, some patients become much worse in this situation.

This brings us to the solutions to the patient's problems, whether the analyst can see them, and whether it will be therapeutically helpful or only cause an unjustified interference to discuss possible solutions with the patient. The following example will, perhaps, make this point clear.

An attractive young woman who, a few years before, had completed four and a half years of full-scale, five-days-a-week analysis came to see an analyst because of a severe state of indecision and confusion which affected all areas of her life. She was undecided as to how to handle her children at mealtime; whether or not to let them have sweets; whether to take them to shows; what to buy them to wear; what clothes to purchase for herself; whether to change the decorating of the house; and so on throughout her life. It soon appeared that she felt compelled to do everything perfectly. This was part of her childhood pattern. It was her way of winning love. With her parents she felt insecure and could assure herself of their acceptance only by perfect behavior. This pattern had been dealt with intensively and extensively in her analysis, but persisted uncorrected. In fact, the patient complained that she was worse now than when she first went for treatment. The situation was clear; she had the insight but was totally unable to use it for therapeutic effect.

In such an instance, should not the analyst take the position that the insight has been achieved and that the central problem is to find inner emotional solutions to discuss with the patient? Freud took the position of helping the patient find solutions when he wrote that psychoanalysis was "after-education" by which the analyst could "correct the parental blunders." What after-education can analysis offer a patient in this young woman's situation?

The analyst imparted to this patient and discussed with her, with therapeutic effect, the following: First, he emphasized that the young woman herself was not neurotic, indecisive, insecure, perfectionist, and the like, but that this was only a part of her childhood pattern; that this was only a part of her personality in sharp contradistinction to the mature part of her makeup; her mature self had good sense of reality, good judgment, was able to marry and have children, to take responsibility for her home, and to relate adequately to people. The first step, in other words, was to separate out the pathodynamic pattern, to make clear what was pathologically infantile and what mature. Several points were involved here: (1) to give her a perspective on her problem; (2) to give her a good image of herself in maturity; and (3) to use the mature part of her ego as a basis for understanding, while keeping the infantile in perspective. In this process we could come back to Freud's original simile of the reclamation of the Zuyder Zee: the task is to build on the mature ego at the expense of the disordered childhood pattern.

The second step continues the first. In this case the obvious realities were pointed out to her. Her husband loved her and she had friends, and not to see this was unrealistic. We understood why she did not: her childhood insecurity in relation to her parents persisted. She was told that there were dynamic reasons as well as historic ones for her feeling and that guilt made her feel that she was unworthy of love. The main point that was emphasized, however, was that her feeling of being unloved was a delusion; and her ideal of perfection had in fact been attained in order to get what, all the time, she actually had.

The third issue discussed with her was the ineffectiveness of the methods she used to get love. Others would not give her love if she was too directly demanding. In reality, the way to get love is not to demand it; this leads to frustration and rejection, and hence to anger and vindictiveness. To get love she should use the mature part of her personality to do a good job with her husband, her children, her friends, and with her community and other activities. One gets love by giving it, not by being perfect or anything else.

In the interest of brevity all the material has not been given, and the three points discussed have been presented in condensed, almost schematic form, to convey the essential; namely, that in many cases the analyst cannot depend on insight alone.

In these cases one of the resources of the analyst is to stop and think what uses he can make of the insight he has gained; one of these is the formulation by the analyst, at first in his own mind, of the patient's essential problem. The second step is for the analyst to think out what the solutions to this problem may be. Naturally, these are not given to the patient in any dogmatic fashion but only after the analyst, in Freud's spirit of after-education, in a face-to-face sitting interview, takes stock and reviews with the patient the nature of the problem and the main dynamics, and then considers the possible solutions. We have not dealt with the supportive, after-educative, corrective effect of the transference and its analysis or with the analyst's personality and the countertransference.

When the analyst makes an interpretation, which comes through to the patient as an infantile image of himself, this interpretation of the patient's infantile quality has behind it the full force of the analyst's authority—of the authority the parents originally had. If the analyst implies that the patient is infantile this must be true, for it repeats what the parents said or implied. To have and to hold the love of the parents is the most important single goal of the young child's life. This same need is the core of the transference. It must be fully recognized by the patient, and the analyst must be aware of its potential for damage.

Actually, the analyst becomes a powerful part of the patient's new superego. The patient through his need for the analyst's love and approval, his fear of the analyst's criticism, accepts the analyst's opinions and interpretations, no matter how devastating. It is unrealistic to think it possible to analyze any patient in such a way that when the analysis ends it is as though the patient never met the analyst. As Freud clearly stated, the analyst has become part of the patient's superego, an influential part of the patient's personality. If he has used his role as the patient's new parent wisely and therapeutically, the residue of the transference is friendly and the patient usually feels warm and grateful toward him. If he has used it badly, there is an undercurrent of resentment for many years and the patient may be unimproved or worse. The patient's original pattern of feelings toward the parents, repeated with the analyst, is never completely outgrown or resolved. However, a diminution may tilt the balance in the patient's life from one of neurotic distress to relative freedom. This is reflected in a countertransference atmosphere that encourages the mature part of the patient's personality to see and to learn to handle and outgrow the disturbing infantile patterns.

Thus, besides giving the patient a realistic self-image which he can validly respect, awareness of the mature part of the patient's personality should be kept in sharp focus because of the nature of analytic treatment. The therapeutic effect of the analytic procedure depends largely on the patient's discriminating between present reality and past patterns which have been derived from the realities of childhood and which interfere with the current mature functioning. Since in the course of the analysis the patient projects his superego onto the analyst, the analyst willy-nilly becomes part of the patient's superego. Insofar as the patient identifies with his parents or is seeking such identification, he will identify himself strongly with his analyst. Therefore, if in making interpretations the analyst unwittingly gives the impression of seeing the patient as an infantile personality, the patient through identification with the analyst is apt to continue this attitude toward himself, reinforced and entrenched rather than corrected.

This is one of the pitfalls of interpretation. If the analyst, focusing upon the infantile reactions, conveys to the patient that this covers the patient *in toto* rather than merely a part of his personality, then even though every interpretation is correct the patient may emerge from the analysis in a beaten-down condition: feeling himself a disturbed, infantile individual rather than one whose total, otherwise adequate personality includes the conflicting inadequacies. The importance of the analyst not conveying any sense of criticism or deprecation in his interpretations, spoken or unspoken, cannot be exaggerated.

REFERENCES

SAUL, L. J. *The Technic and Practice of Psychoanalysis.* Philadelphia: J. B. Lippincott, 1958.

Remarks on Success and Failure in Psychoanalysis and Psychotherapy

EDWARD GLOVER, M.D., LL. D.,: F.B.P.S.

THE PRACTICE of stock-taking in science, in other words of registering from time to time any notable changes that may have taken place in a given field of observation, is as difficult as it is laudable. It is laudable insofar as it provides students and qualified investigators with a convenient digest of recent work on the subject; but if and when this digest is supplemented by an assessment of the significance and trend of the changes, it is very difficult indeed. When, for example, may a change be considered an advance, a backsliding, or merely a state of *transition* without any definite line of direction? Who can guess whether or not any alleged transition points in a definite direction?

The topic of Success and Failure in Psychoanalysis and Psychotherapy is, I think, bound to stir a hornet's nest of controversial issues—if not among the contributors to this volume, at any rate among different "schools" of readers. What, for example, are the standards of success and failure; or, going a little deeper, what are the criteria of interpretation on which these standards are based? In the case of psychoanalysis it is pretty clear that these are not merely clinical but also depend on the theories of mental function maintained by any given psychoanalyst. Is there then a reasonably substantial consensus on analytical theories? If not, then statistical records of therapeutic results should be subject to a scale of theoretical values.

Pursuing this line, one is bound to inquire as to the nature of the statistical records. What clinical scales were applied and what were the standards of selection of cases; what was the original prognosis; what statistical controls, if any, were employed; what was the length of treatment and of the after-history; how far are the records of different observers comparable; and, of course, not only what variety of technique was adopted but is the range of techniques comparable with different observers? In short, considering this one item alone, it seems clear that *the process of recording results calls for the use of criteria drawn from a very wide range of the theories and practices of analysts.* Stated in the most general terms this means that when stock-taking includes appraisal and direction-finding *the most stringent safeguards are required to prevent gross error.* Appraisal is after all a form of analytic synthesis and calls for as broad an understanding and as refined a technique as does therapeutic analysis itself. And although it ill becomes me to dogmatize about general psychotherapy, I should have said that *mutatis mutandis,* the same or very similar principles should apply to that more widely distributed form of mental therapy.

At this point the logical course would seem to be to catalogue, examine, and illustrate the numerous pitfalls, uncertainties, and sources of error which surround and thereby obscure the meaning of terms such as "psychotherapeutic success" or "failure." But in view of the foregoing considerations I think we would do better to return to the first term of reference and consider more closely the implications of the word "transition." To be sure our dictionaries are prepared to accept in exchange such generalizations as "change" or "passage"; on the other hand, they are pretty emphatic that the word implies a change from one place or state or act or set of circumstances *to another*. Now, that is precisely what cannot be said of the great majority of changes heralded by modern clinical psychology and in particular of the theories spun and marketed by ambitious psychoanalysts, for, on the whole, general psychologists do not possess and therefore cannot market theories of mental function, whereas psychoanalysts are under obligation to live up to their basic principles.

Herein lies one of the difficulties peculiar to psychoanalytical assessments. The validity of an analytical theory of assessment depends not on its (pre)conscious form, however elaborate that may be, but on the degree to which it is consonant with the basic principles of the science. Metapsychology, to use that rather ambiguous term, is concerned for the most part with the unconscious functions that govern mental activity.

Ever since the nineteen-thirties and more particularly since the death of Freud, an increasing number of attempts have been made in this and other countries to modify or extend Freudian theory and consequently analytical systems of assessment. And these have been hailed by their authors and his or her followers as "advances" fortifying and extending the scope of psychoanalysis. But the price to be paid for most of these alleged advances is a heavy one, leading to erroneous estimations and uncertain clinical standards. This is easy to understand; for if a new set of conceptions, however disguised in Freudian terminology, should happen to be erroneous, its exercise is bound to affect clinical estimations of, for example, success or failure.

One party may maintain that a clinical failure was due to neglect in applying the new ideas; another that it was due to their application. Therefore, before evaluating "transitions" it is necessary to prove that a state of transition actually exists, and that whatever ideational or clinical form it takes does not depart from the basic concepts on which psychoanalysis was founded.

It should be remembered that although Freud was indeed a great revolutionary and ready to make changes where he felt they were called for, he was also and rightly a great conservative and held tenaciously to his fundamental concepts.

To come back after this digression to the subject in hand, I doubt whether in the passage of millennia any fundamental change in the concepts of transference and countertransference will occur. I am convinced these manifestations will not materially alter and that the handling, mishandling, or neglect of these psychic states will still provide sovereign standards by which to distinguish psychoanalytic from general psychotherapy, a matter of no small import when one is considering the nature of alleged transitions and the rationale of success or failure in psychotherapy.

STANDARDS OF SUCCESS
AND FAILURE

So much, then, for a rough preliminary consideration of principles. The task remains, however, to set in order the standards by which one can assess the success or failure of any psychotherapeutic effort. And it seems to me that the best way to avoid confusion on this subject is to follow the clinical history of the analytical relationship in any given case from consultation to discharge, finally recording the after-history for the benefit of statisticians. It should be assumed, however, that the following considerations apply to the practice of psychoanalysis. Occasional references to general psychotherapy will be earmarked as such.

The Selection of Cases

To those therapists who are accustomed to regulating their case intake in accordance with more sober and restricted categories, such as diagnosis and prognosis, the emphasis laid on the term "selection" would seem to call for some justification. Yet it is essential to note that nowadays the ultimate selection of cases is regulated by more *individual and subjective standards than formerly*. In the earlier days of psychoanalysis this source of error in estimation was not so obvious. Psychoanalysis as a clinical science was based mostly on the observation of the psychoneuroses which provided a model for the study of symptom-formation. But as time went on, the range of therapy came to include such conditions as psychoses, cases of character disorder, sexual perversion, social maladaptations of a psychopathic nature, and the like. Consequently, both diagnosis and prognosis depended more on the experience and prejudices of the observer than on well-established clinical distinctions. And not only on the experience of the observer, but on the scope of his professional training.

For example, where no specific training in general psychiatry is obligatory, two antithetical reactions may be observed. Either the practitioner tends to fight shy of undertaking the analysis of psychotic types or he is prepared to undertake the analysis of such cases without any clear understanding of their difficulty. And the same goes for the analysis of character disorders and other conditions more intractable than the psychoneuroses. Not only so, it seems to be the case that whereas candidates in training may be lucky enough to cut their teeth on relatively easy cases, practitioners who advance in seniority tend to find their case lists loaded with disorders of an intractable nature, many of which have gone from pillar to post under the care of a variety of therapists of every description.

In such instances terms such as "success" or "failure" are clearly inadequate, because they are "dependent variables." It would be absurd to maintain that because a case seems to be difficult, intractable, or at best capable only of slight improvement it should therefore be denied analytic treatment. Organic physicians do not countenance for a moment such high-handed, arbitrary, and rather cowardly policies. Yet if no improvement or only a minor degree of improvement ensues, is that to be recorded as a "failure"? To be sure, the onus should lie on the diagnostic and prognostic skill of the consultant, who should of course forewarn or advise the prospective patient of the possible outcome of his treatment, whether favorable or unfavorable. The ultimate result can be recorded under the usual headings of "cured," "much improved," "improved," "*in statu quo*," "worse," or "much worse"; but so long as the treatment has followed sound lines there is no reason for the analyst to repine. If we must use such moralistic or respectively pejorative captions as "success" and "failure," let us at least distinguish between "honorable failure" and "failure due to inadequacies in diagnosis, prognosis, and treatment." And while we are at it, let us not be too cocky about success. Any analyst knows that some of his greatest "successes" ("cures") are achieved with a minimum of analytic effort and in a surprisingly short space of time. (General psychotherapists, please copy.)

Of course, it is easy to understand why psychoanalysts were, and I think still are, cagey about their therapeutic results. For since 1893, they have been subject to denigration and vituperation from a covey of normal psychologists, neurologists, and critics at large. But they have no reason to be discouraged. After all, the progress of any science depends to a considerable extent on the careful examination of what I have called "honorable failures." What the timid analyst or anyone who professes to treat mental disorder should avoid is the reactive tendency to recommend for treatment, be it analytical or nonanalytical, everyone who consults him, irrespective of diagnosis, prognosis, and the nature of exciting causes; for this policy sooner or later will lead to frustration and discouragement.

Variations in Technique and Theory of Technique

Having maintained that a prerequisite of accurate estimations of the results of any given system of psychotherapy (a necessary preliminary to the study of "success" and "failure") is the existence of a more or less standardized technique accepted and followed by a substantial majority of practitioners, let us assume that a case has been duly selected for treatment. It would then seem logical to inquire whether in the case of psychoanalytic treatment these prerequisites have been duly satisfied, or whether variations in technique are remarkable enough to suggest the existence of a transition in development, whether or not the direction of this change can be specified. To fullfil this logical requirement would obviously necessitate a detailed review of the whole practice and theory of psychoanalysis, and this is scarcely practicable within the limitations of a symposium. Nevertheless, some of the more outstanding forms of variation deserve to be singled out. Briefly, the main possibilities are (1) that the standard technique has been followed and that such variations as can be observed merely reflect changes necessitated in the handling of special cases that do not fall within the range of classical psychoneuroses, or their equivalents; (2) that the classical techniques are interspersed with variations to such a degree as to suggest a deviation from accepted psychoanalytical principles; (3) that the variations are dictated by the analyst's compulsion to exploit esoteric theories that clearly deviate from accepted analytical principles.

As far as the first two standards are concerned, in a "Questionnaire Research on Technique" I was able to establish [1] that although a majority subscribed to standard analytical techniques there were very few points, excepting that of transference-analysis, on which a full consensus existed. Considerable variations in practice were obvious, and in the case of a minority these were so striking as to suggest a third possibility: that some fundamental change in the theory of psychoanalysis had been or was about to be canonized as a new but essential part of psychoanalytical theory.[2]

This appeared to me to be a crucial issue and I decided to follow the matter up, using as a test case the criteria of interpretation, which by common consent constitute one of the few standard features of orthodox

[1] Originally published as An Investigation of the Technique of Psycho-analysis, 1940. Subsequently revised, slightly abridged, and incorporated in E. Glover, *The Technique of Psycho-analysis.* London: Bailliere, Tindall, and Cassell, 1955.

[2] This suspicion was confirmed when, after almost two years of acrimonious but completely sterile debate, the British Psycho-Analytical Society organized two distinct systems of training for candidates: a Freudian system and a Kleinian system. This barely concealed dichotomy persists to the present day.

psychoanalysis. The conclusion seemed to me to be obvious: [3] that *when any two analysts or groups of analysts hold diametrically opposed views on interpretation, mental mechanisms, or content, one of them must inevitably practice the technique of suggestion rather than that of psychoanalysis.* Following this lead, I embarked on a survey of all the technical devices that enable a clear distinction to be drawn between psychoanalytical therapy and "general psychotherapy." [4] The conclusions arrived at in this more extended survey supported those arrived at in the paper, "Inexact Interpretation." There appeared to be 24 factors by which one could hope to distinguish between analytic and nonanalytic psychotherapy. Of these, some six could be described as "metapsychological criteria," of which four at least were a source of controversy. Five could be described as clinical (psychopathological) standards, of which three at least were controversial; 12 were concerned with methodology, of which nine involved diametrically opposed theories of mental function.

---

[3] Originally published as The Therapeutic Effect of Inexact Interpretation, in *International Journal of Psychoanalysis,* 1931, **12:** 397. Reprinted in Glover, *op. cit.*

[4] Originally published as Therapeutic Criteria of Psycho-analysis, in *International Journal of Psychoanalysis,* 1954, **33:** Part 2. Reprinted in Glover, *op. cit.*

See also The Indications for Psycho-analysis, originally published in Journal of Mental Science, 1954, **100:** No. 419. Reprinted in E. Glover, *On the Early Development of Mind.* London: Allen and Unwin, 1956.

Psychotherapeutic Standards

At this point it is easy to surmise the reaction of those psychotherapists who are by nature refractory to psychoanalytical formulations. They will say, "Well, what did we tell you? Psychoanalysis is confessedly a broken reed," forgetting that judged by the same standards there is no form of general psychotherapy which could not be attacked. This is, by the way, a little ungrateful of them, for the point I wish to emphasize is, first, that the validity of theory cannot be established by therapeutic results. Because an advanced schizophrenic does not respond to analytic treatment, that in no way contradicts the theories of schizophrenic reaction advanced by psychoanalysts.

On the other hand, the common assumption that a favorable therapeutic result (a "success") establishes the validity of the theory on which the treatment was based is equally unsafe. An inexact system of interpretations based on theories which in important respects run counter to established analytical principles does not prove the analytical soundness of the theories. For if, as I maintain, a favorable outcome in such cases is due to the exploitation of suggestion, the result should be recorded not as an outcome of psychoanalysis but of general psychotherapy. In other words, the terms "success" or "failure" are dependent variables, ill-adapted to the assessment of results and the valuation of theoretical systems.

Of course, it can be argued that the same applies to

more elaborate classifications such as the customary series: "cured," "much improved," "improved," *"in statu quo,"* "worse," and "much worse"; that without due control in terms of diagnosis, prognosis, selection, and technique these, too, are not very helpful to research. But at least they are more elastic and more easily checked for error. For, as has been pointed out, a marginal improvement in a difficult or intractable case though seemingly a "failure" deserves to be rated a "success." And incidentally these difficult cases are not confined to psychotic, characterological or psychosexual groups but are to be found also in psychoneurotic groups; as, for example, in the monosymptomatic anxiety phobias and in those cases of obsessional neurosis which are superimposed on an underlying paranoid or depressive substructure.

But whichever system of classification is adopted, there is yet another source of variation, namely, in the *clinical systems* employed to assess results. Exception is sometimes taken to relying mainly on symptomatic standards. And it is certainly true that effective diagnosis and prognosis depend on examination of the mental apparatus as a whole, the function of the total personality, as it used to be called. But in the majority of cases, that is not what brings the patient to consultation: he complains of symptoms, and desires to be "cured" (rid) of them. If after the examination you decide to recommend psychoanalysis, he will, unless you specify to the contrary, expect to be "cured." I have in the past only too frequently heard an analyst say of a patient who had proved difficult that although on discharge he still manifested "symptom remainders" (an intriguing euphemism), he was much improved in other respects. True enough, no doubt, but not what the patient wanted; in other words, a partial if not total "failure."

Following this line of argument one ought, strictly speaking, to examine every type of symptom, every technical device, every mental mechanism, and every analytical phase or situation which might either support or vitiate assessments of the end result (success or failure). But I think it will be sufficient to consider two more of the essential factors. The first of these runs under various headings: "resistances," "negative transferences," and "negative therapeutic reactions"; and the second concerns the duration of analysis and the clinical phase in which it is terminated; or perhaps it would be better to say the point at which the patient is either discharged or discharges himself.

Now, according to Freud's classification, transference resistance is one of three main ego-resistances, the others being defense (contra-id) resistance and resistance due to the "gains through illness" (both "primary" and "secondary"). The term "negative therapeutic reaction," which soon became and still enjoys a considerable vogue, was identified as "superego resistance," when guilt conflict with the ego gives rise to the persistent exploitation of symptoms as a form of self-punishment. This, after id resistance, was held to be the most intractable of reactions. And when to these subdivisions are added their appropriate counterparts (counter resistances harbored by the analyst), the total list is flexible enough to comprise the main factors responsible for degrees of failure in treatment.

But unfortunately technical terms sometimes become clichés and can be exploited in professional defense against partial or total failure. This seems to have been the case with the term "negative therapeutic reaction," which in any event lacks specificity and can function as a kind of extenuation of *any* form of resistance that for one reason or another obstructs therapeutic progress. And this greatly reduces the value of factorial assessments of either progress or regress. For even if such excuses are valid, the onus is still on the analyst to strengthen his own diagnostic and prognostic criteria. One ought not blame the patient for absence of efficient diagnosis.[5]

The second essential factor—the duration of analysis and the state of mind of the patient at the time when either he is discharged or discharges himself—adds considerably to the difficulties of factorial assessment of the "results" of analytic psychotherapy. In the old days, the duration of analysis either of patients or of candidates in training was comparatively short, sometimes only a few months. Yet it was on the strength of these early quick-fire assessments that psychoanalysis was able to force itself on the therapeutic scene. In these modern times, when analysis may stretch from a

---

[5] A similar reaction could be observed in the earlier days of psychoanalysis, when lack of success was sometimes condoned by the analyst responsible for it on the ground that the patient proved to be "too narcissistic" or "schizoid" or just a "psychotic character." This apology was naturally advanced most frequently by analysts with little or no psychiatric experience.

two-year average to interminable analysis (15–20 years), one is bound to consider whether the early results were dependable or the later standards unconscionable.

Not only so, it was never quite certain when any one analysis could be regarded as "finished," though why this theoretical standard should be applied is not at all clear. That there is a terminal phase to analysis theoretically is a plausible proposition, in which case the obvious course for the analyst to follow in difficult cases is to warn his patient beforehand that, whether after treatment he is better or not, he cannot expect more from this obviously promising form of therapy. Termination is in my opinion an arbitrary standard. I believe that there is indeed a terminal phase, but I think also that this is seldom reached. After all, patients do tend to follow their own destiny, whatever the analyst may feel is desirable for them.

This situation is most clearly established in the case of the psychoanalysis of children. I do not for a moment believe that child analysis is ever terminated. And obviously what is sauce for the gosling is sauce for the post pubertal semi-adult or full-blown adult. One must face the fact that if an analysis is not terminated *secundum artem,* it cannot claim to be more than a highly specialized form of general psychotherapy. To be sure, there is a fundamental difference between the ideal psychoanalysis and ideal general psychotherapy, in that practitioners of general psychotherapy need not consider the existence of unconscious mental functions and therefore can with a good conscience ignore the infinite and often inextricable complexity and confusion of mental processes. He can, if he so wishes, apply the flattering unction to his soul that his compost of eclectic maneuvers from lobotomy or mesial section of the brain hemispheres to religious reassurance represents the acme of human psychotherapeutic endeavor. (Profound indeed must be the peace of mind of the happy eclectic.) But let us return to clinical realities.

A Case of Psychoanalytical Confusion

Here I am tempted to interpolate a thumbnail sketch of a case referred to me almost half a century ago, when I was an analytic sophomore. I have often quoted it to illustrate the hazards of diagnostic, prognostic, and therapeutic standards of assessment. Briefly, this was the case of a young man in his early twenties, who was sent to me labeled as a "typical case of obsessional neurosis," a diagnosis which seemed to me at the time entirely justified. His analysis therefore proceeded according to the accustomed psychoanalytical plan up to the point where his defenses against an inverted Oedipus situation blocked any further progress. At the end of two months he informed me that his symptoms seemed to be evaporating and he finally told me that he was satisfied with his treatment and therefore felt there was no point in continuing it. This coincided with a decision to set up house with his widowed mother with whom he had previously had a markedly ambivalent relationship. Naturally, in accordance with conventional social standards, we parted with expressions of mutual esteem. But it so happened that I was able to follow his after-history throughout a period of almost 30 years. He had, he assured me, never had the slightest recurrence of his obsessional trouble and had pursued a conflict-free life up to the time when his mother died, when he suffered a mild reactive depression of a temporary nature.

Later I attempted to record the results of this casual analytic treatment in terms of success or failure. I decided that analytically speaking he was a "failure." Even psychiatrically regarded, no particular evidence existed that his improvement could be accounted for on general psychiatric grounds. The fact appeared to be that with more than a touch of therapeutic genius he combined his defenses with and sustained in practice a tempered compromise with his primary unconscious wishes and guilts. Under the stimulus of an existing and potentially dangerous analytic situation, he achieved a spontaneous remission of his original symptoms. One can't help wondering how often analysts designate as "successes" the spontaneous defenses and solutions of conflict developed by patients themselves. Thirty years, after all, is quite a time. He must now be well into his sixties, symptom-free and with no grudge against some obvious inhibitions, a harness that kept his id in happy subjection.

Variations in Scientific Records: The After-History

The foregoing clinical sketch may serve to bring us back to the essential issue. No doubt it would be easy to elaborate a supplementary list of factors by which to list the success or failure of psychotherapeutic techniques, whatever their nature. The fact remains, however, that in the instance described what at first sight might have been taken to be a psychoanalytical success (highly approved of by the patient) was actually a psychoanalytical failure, and very possibly not even a "general psychotherapeutic" success. The moral would appear to be that, unless carefully screened for error, very few psychotherapeutic records would pass muster as scientific data or conclusions.

This, of course, is not of itself a criticism of the technical methods adopted in any given case, whether psychoanalytic or simply generally psychotherapeutic in nature. But I think it does indicate the pressing need to control all therapeutic records, insofar as that is humanly possible. And it suggests that the final test of any psychological approach to the amelioration of mental disorder must lie with a carefully screened after-history.

But how many present-day after-history records would pass muster? To take a simple instance: It seems clear that a final after-history should be based on as meticulous a clinical examination of the patient as was carried out when he first came to consultation. Naturally, it is not possible to arrange such careful surveys in every case. But that does not enhance the validity of postal surveys provided by the nearest interested party, including sometimes the ex-patient himself. Moreover, the date when an after-history may be regarded as final is quite unsettled. A *minimum* of five years seems to be indicated; but the longer the better, provided in the meantime no traumatic developments in life or love have disturbed the record, and provoked "legitimate" relapses. After-history is after all not so conclusive as it sounds and often seems to be capricious. To take one more clinical instance based on psychoanalytical experience: study of patients who for one personal circumstance or another have been compelled to "break off" analysis shows that, provided the curative process has been set in train, improvement may continue during the subsequent six to twelve months after the break; sometimes much longer.

This is all very perplexing and unsettling, but I do not think that, in a minority of cases, it can be gainsaid. To be sure, it would be foolishly sanguine to *depend* on this manifestation of analytical "momentum," just as it would be foolishly pessimistic to deny the spontaneous "movement" in analysis that may occur once the "analytical situation" has been well established. And so long as no attempt is made by the analyst to shelter uncertainties behind sanguine expectations no exception can be taken. Some elasticity in judgment must be permitted the bona fide clinical observer; even the hardiest statistician who ventures to manipulate clinical records must admit that his own findings depend in the long run on the degree to which his informants temper their assessments with balanced judgment and perspective.

PROVISIONAL CONCLUSIONS

So far our attention has been focused mainly on the issue of the methodology of psychotherapy using for

this purpose the particular case of psychoanalytic therapy and concentrating on the possible sources of error
that may distort the definition and use of labels such
as "success" and "failure." But if we hark back to
whether or not psychotherapy is in a "state of
transition"—i.e., "advancing,"—this issue, in turn,
seems to depend on whether or not fresh observations
or new theories have developed that justify and pro-
mote new techniques.

But before attempting to submit any provisional
conclusions regarding both of these issues, I should
like to say that regardless of the internecine conflict
between psychological "schools," and there is no doubt
that it exists, the question is simply whether all or any
of these schools are advancing or have become linked
up with adventitious non-psychological sciences. I have
written almost exclusively of psychoanalysis because it
is the psychological method based on theories of mental function to which I cleave tenaciously in my practice. Further, I would suggest that there is evidence of
"change" in either general psychotherapy or in psychoanalysis. Consider briefly two examples, viz., group
therapy and narcotherapy, sometimes called group
analysis and narcoanalysis, respectively. Actually, both
of these are legitimate expansions of general psychotherapy, although it would be more accurate to call
the first sociotherapy. But despite the use of the term
"group analysis," this technique has not the remotest
connection with pscyhoanalysis. And narcoanalysis, although a legitimate form of general psychotherapy, is
simply a neurologically based adjuvant to the tech-

nique of hypnotism or suggestion. It has no specific analytic basis.

This argument could be extended to include all varieties of neurosurgery, or pharmacological treatment, from the most cardinal brain operations to the administration of aspirin at the beginning of an attack of migraine. It all depends on what is meant by "psycho"-therapy. If this term means simply the treatment of psychic disorders, there is nothing to argue about. Hitting the patient on the head with a hammer or drenching him with a pail of iced water (clearly the maiden aunts of modern shock therapy) would then pass as psychotherapy. If, however, the term psychotherapy means *treating mental disorders by psychological devices,* the fact must be faced that apart from one revolutionary development now about 75 years old nothing psychologically new or advanced has been promoted. There has, of course, been a great deal of *"avant-garde"* talk, and a plentitude of old and rather superficial ideas tricked out in an apparently new terminology. In a way, that is inevitable—dealcoholized wine in new bottles with fresh labels. Bowdlerization seems to me to be the destiny of general psychotherapy. In the case of psychoanalysis there is also a good deal of self-satisfied talk about "advances" in theory and, although not quite so frequently, about "advances" in technique. But in spite of considerable ballyhoo in several countries, there is little sign of advance in psychoanalytical theory and still less in technique.

Which leads me once more to what in my view is the real problem of alleged "transitional" phases:

namely, is the direction of the "transition" forward or backward? Progress or regress? Not just regress to simpler formulations, but a departure or deviation from the main principles of psychoanalysis. During an active canvassing of the problem of terminating an analysis, Freud once remarked that the best way to terminate it was to carry it out correctly. This is the type of conservative maxim that all "transitionalists" might well take to heart.

Somato-psychic Interaction as Seen in Treatment Failures in a Mental Hospital

HENRY BRILL, M.D.

IN THE course of well over three decades of mental hospital practice I have seen my share of treatment failures. In view of the fact that most of my work involved the use of somatic modalities in combination with psychotherapeutic ones, it is not surprising that in virtually all of them the interaction of psyche and soma has appeared to play a prominent role.

The same principles are, of course, to be seen in therapeutic successes but not in such a convincing fashion because success is extraordinarily difficult to define under conditions of ordinary clinical practice. It is almost impossible to rule out spontaneous recovery; moreover, patients who look recovered in the consulting room may not make such a favorable impression at work or at home; the therapist may be happier with the treatment outcome than are the patient's family, employer, or the patient himself, which raises many more questions in relation to success.

It is ironical, but true, that failure is more clear-cut and unequivocal and does not, like success, require the proofs of scientific controls and instruments of quantification. A suicide, a catastrophic relapse, or a serious overt act usually leaves few doubts that a treatment failure has occurred. This may be the reason why we learn more from our failures than from our successes, or it may be that we think more about them. Regardless of the reason, several cases of therapeutic failure stand out more clearly in my recollection than do any of those who recovered; these failures seem to illustrate principles of psychsomatic unity in a particularly convincing way. This must, in part at least, be a function of my own point of view, yet I am convinced that much more is involved. Let me outline several of these cases.

A Catatonic Relapse

The first was a young single man, admitted in a catatonic state, semi-stuporous and tense. As a clerk in a civil service position he had led a quiet life, which was finally interrupted by a severe schizophrenic episode with catatonic and paranoid features. He responded well to a course of insulin shock therapy, became active on the ward, was well liked by all, and obviously benefited from a series of sessions of supportive psychotherapy. He was unusually philosophical about his continued stay in the hospital; in retrospect he was perhaps too philosophical.

Finally the day came when we were making plans for his release and then we found that he had no close family ties on which to rely. Nevertheless, in spite of his schizophrenic illness and his schizoid personality, he did have a girl friend who was very anxious to help him. He contacted her somewhat reluctantly, and after that matters moved rapidly. Then a new development occurred, even more surprising. He had not one but two girl friends, both equally interested in him. We took no part in this situation, although we noted a degree of concern and ambivalence in him. For a time, the two girls visited him on different days and all seemed to be going well. Then, on one visiting day I was called to the ward on an emergency. Both ladies were in the visiting room and he was sitting between them, almost mute, confused, and perspiring so profusely that my associate and I were forced to rule out a relapse into hypoglycemic coma, although it was totally unbelievable that he could have suffered any kind of late secondary hypoglycemia, as it had been weeks since he had had his last insulin. Yet he looked exactly as he did when he was going into a usual insulin coma, perspiring profusely, confused, and out of contact with the outer world. A liberal injection of intravenous glucose was without effect, and we were forced to admit that under maximum emotional stress he had suffered full catatonic relapse with the additional feature of profuse perspiration to an extent which I never saw before or since in a catatonic stupor. Subsequently, he was given another full course of insulin, and I made strenuous attempts to reach him psychotherapeutically—all to no avail.

When I last saw him some years later, he remained catatonic, tense, withdrawn, and somewhat depressed. The perspiration occurred only on the day of the acute episode with the two ladies; subsequently the catatonia was not unusual in any way. The relapse obviously involved dynamic factors; perhaps we could have avoided the relapse if we had warned him against the double entanglement more explicitly, or perhaps even against a single involvement. Perhaps he should have avoided both girls, and we might have persuaded him to delay all action till the indications were clearer. Yet the somatic aspects were so prominent that I have never been able to shake off the feeling that somehow they contributed to the depth of his reaction.

Resolution of Amnesia

A second case, with a curious interweaving of psychic and somatic elements, occupied a number of us for some months. The case was that of a young man, admitted in a catatonic state, and selectively amnesic for all data which could have established his identity. Under a course of insulin shock therapy, the schizophrenic symptoms cleared, leaving a pleasant, outgoing, lively, and somewhat manipulative young man who made quite an impression on some of the female personnel.

He had recovered completely from the catatonia, but the amnesia remained and was untouched by all subsequent efforts. We used sodium amytal in a modified hypnotic technique, free associations, examination of dream content, and word associations designed to identify at least some of his background. Finally he willingly underwent a course of metrazol treatments in an effort to recall—all to no avail.

Noteworthy was the fact that all psychotherapeutic efforts were a flat failure in an area where it is usually so simple, namely in overcoming a nonorganic amnesia. A single "hysterical" symptom resisted all somatic therapy, although the more malignant symptoms had cleared quickly. We were finally forced to release him from the hospital, still amnesic but otherwise in a good condition. He appealed to the press for help but the published pictures brought no response. Finally I was commissioned to join him in New York, "to do something" to resolve the embarrassment in various quarters, which now mounted daily.

My confidence was at a low point, but having no choice I put him and two reporters in my car and ordered him to select the direction of travel by free association. He protested but the traffic in New York added urgency to a situation of forced choices, and with mounting confidence he did in reality what he had failed to do in fantasy on many trials: He navigated the car to his home. We had tried this repeatedly in the hospital and he had failed completely, but confronted with free choice in an actual reality situation he succeeded.

I did not see this as a success by psychotherapeutic methods; rather it was a failure at the psychotherapeutic level. Success came when he faced a reality situation. The family situation, incidentally, made his amnesia somewhat more comprehensible once we saw what he faced in that quarter. He had left home on previous occasions and shortly afterward I received a card from him, again on the road. His family had seen the press notices but had not come forward, knowing the past record and anticipating future events.

Lobar Pneumonia

A third case involved psychosomatics, in a spectacular fashion. A male employee of about 40 was in sickbay with lobar pneumonia. It was in the days before serum was in general clinical use, and antibiotics were only a Utopian dream. Medical treatment was limited to nursing care, supportive medication, and oxygen, and a form of supportive psychotherapy was recognized as a key issue in treatment; the usual experience was that once the patient had lost hope and confidence, a fatal outcome was virtually assured.

The patient was on the mend, with falling temperature and a sense of well-being that augured well. Then came a visit from an authoritative figure who harangued him without mercy on an ethical issue. An emergency call from the ward was too late. I failed to relieve his emotional state; his temperature shot up within the hour and a spectacular deterioration of his physical condition followed. Within 36 hours he was dead. I have always wondered if he would have lived if I had maintained protection for his psychic state.

A Somato-psychic Reaction

The final case appears to be a clear-cut somato-psychic reaction. On one of our wards in the early 1930s was a woman with a cerebellar tumor that was considered inoperable. She was querulous, complaining, demanding, difficult, and given to bouts of screaming and to paranoid projections. Early one day she demanded to see the priest to get the last rites. I

examined her and found no change and no indication
for calling the priest, who at that time was miles away.
Firmly and gently I explained that the Father would
be by to see her as soon as feasible. Her response was
hostile and vigorous, not that of a dying woman. My
reassurance was firm, protracted, and full of confidence, and finally she listened. At dusk the Catholic
chaplain arrived. We asked him to see her, and she re-
quested him to administer the last rites. Hardly had he
finished, when her condition changed and I watched
her die during the next two hours. I was so incredu-
lous that I checked my findings by ophthalmoscope
and actually saw the blood in the retinal vessels break
into segments in typical fashion. This was perhaps a
failure of evaluation in the first instance, but it also involved a failure in an approach to alleviate tension and
anxiety.

What can we make of these observations, which incidentally are each examples of a class, rather than isolated instances? To me they are instances of different
types of interaction of psyche and soma, and provide
another line of evidence on a descriptive level that the
distinction between somatic and psychic events is
often, and may usually be, unwarranted.

The principle of psychosomatic unity is often mentioned and in itself is not all new. Yet the cases which
have been outlined seem to illustrate the principle in a
sufficiently striking fashion to warrant recording them
here.

The Fear of Compassion[1]

Arnold Bernstein, Ph.D.

THIS BRIEF presentation might well have been titled, "On being human, though a psychoanalyst," for in it I intend to discuss psychoanalysts' reluctance to meet with simple human feelings the suffering they witness in their patients, irrespective of the source of such misery. I attribute this state of affairs to what psychoanalysts call reaction formation, and to the development in them of a countertransference *resistance* to feeling compassion.

Human compassion is, I believe, an emotion singularly human and singularly civilized, and probably the last, or at least among the last emotions to have evolved during the long phylogenesis of the human psyche. Tradition has it that compassion is almost "god-like," forming no small part of modern man's religious heritage. Only lately and after much suffering and resistance has pitilessness in human relations begun to yield to pity and compassion, but even a casual review of the extensive cruelties that still characterize human behavior confirms that the evolution of compassion among men is still far from complete.

Like mankind in the beginning, each particular

[1] Portions of this chapter appeared in A. Bernstein, The Problem of Transference in Psychoanalysts. *Psychoanalysis and the Psychoanalytic Review*, 1958, **45**: 86–91.

human being is born without the capacity to experience the feeling of compassion and acquires this ability, if at all, as a result of a socialization process which renders him a mature adult person. For better or for worse, in one sense or another, psychological *ontogenesis* (development of individual personality) often recapitulates cultural *phylogenesis* (evolution of a cultural group). Neither animals nor children are truly compassionate. Indeed, compassion seems to be among the attributes that mark a person as being capable of mature love. Compassion bears a relation to the affectionate component of love analogous to the relation that genitality bears to the sensual component. Infantile love is neither compassionate nor genital. On the contrary, parental love requires both of these components to be present. It would not be stretching the point too far to suggest that transference love in a patient is comparable to the former, and countertransference love in a psychoanalyst is comparable to the latter.

A naive and literal misreading of Freud has perpetuated two ubiquitous and compelling psychoanalytic shibboleths, both of which conspire to deprive psychoanalysts of the privilege of enjoying their feelings, especially the feeling of compassion, and of the option of behaving compassionately with respect to their patients. The shibboleths are the fear of "countertransference" and the "abstinence rule." I am inclined to attribute many treatment failures to the prohibition against compassionate behavior on the part of psychoanalysts that misapplication of these two principles has led to. In support of this contention I shall later report my first and most dramatic treatment failure. I credit this failure to my inability or unwillingness to act compassionately toward a patient. This inability was a result of previous indoctrination regarding the handling of countertransference and the implementation of the abstinence rule. I shall also report an equally dramatic success which followed when I threw off my inhibitions in these matters and acted as a compassionate human being.

Although Freud (1910) makes only a passing reference to "the countertransference" as a problem in psychoanalysis, his brief comment on this issue has had a persisting influence on psychoanalytic practice, supervision, and training. The countertransference, Freud says, "arises in the physician as a result of the patient's influence on his unconscious feelings." He recommends that a psychoanalyst "recognize and overcome this countertransference in himself." For a psychoanalyst's "achievement is limited by what his own complexes and resistances permit." Accordingly he should practice self-analysis and "should extend and deepen this constantly while making his observations on his patients. Anyone who cannot succeed in this self-analysis may without more ado regard himself as unable to treat neurotics by analysis."

The nub of these remarks is that psychoanalysts should not be victimized by their own complexes and resistances but should be constantly on the alert through self-monitoring against *"unconscious* feelings" that might interfere with their freedom to conduct a successful analysis. The crux of the matter is not the psychoanalyst's feelings but the psychoanalyst's resistances. It is a travesty that this interdiction *against resistance* has itself been transposed *into* a resistance against feelings. For it is precisely a psychoanalyst's resistance to recognizing his own feelings that Freud identifies as the countertransference problem. The clearest evidence of countertransference resistance is an inability or unwillingness on the part of a psychoanalyst to experience normal and appropriate feelings when these are called for and when these might usefully serve a patient and advance an analysis.

It appears to me to be necessary to discriminate between unresolved transferences in a psychoanalyst, countertransference feelings, and what might more properly be called countertransference resistances. It is no new thought that I am setting forth here, that countertransference feelings need not constitute an impediment for a psychoanalyst but may in fact be utilized by him as a potent source of analytic material with which to further treatment.

My contention is that if an analyst is a healthy, mature, gentle human being, his human response to the expression of a need for help on the part of another human being is a feeling of compassion. Compassion is the socially complementary role response to a child or to a person in need of help or to any living creature in pain.

In the face of a patient's transference demand "Help me!" an analyst must and should feel the countertransference response of compassion. Unfortunately, a misreading of the countertransference prohibition makes analysts, or at least young analysts and beginning analysts, afraid of having *any* feelings. Instead of responding to a patient's demand for help by feeling compassion, analysts all too frequently renounce such normal feelings in favor of countertransference resistance. Thus, instead of feeling compassion in the face of a patient's demand to "Help me!" they feel coldness, objectivity, and withdrawal.

The fear of countertransference feelings derives powerful sustenance from still another source. In 1912, Freud advised: "I cannot recommend my colleagues emphatically enough to take as a model in psychoanalytic treatment the surgeon who puts aside all his own feelings, including that of human sympathy, and concentrates his mind on one single purpose, that of performing the operation as skillfully as possible."

Such an unequivocal and emphatic declaration hardly seems to lend itself to any but the literal interpretation that psychoanalysts have placed upon it, namely to eschew all feelings during the conduct of treatment. But to more fully appreciate Freud's advice on this matter requires a thoughtful appraisal of the reasons he sets forth for his conclusion. It is not the psychoanalyst's compassionate impulses that Freud elects to indict but, he says, "the affective impulse of greatest danger will be the therapeutic ambition to achieve . . . something which will impress and convince others." Moreover, Freud explains, "The justification for this coldness in feeling in the analyst is that it is the condition which brings the greatest advantage to both persons involved, ensuring a needful protection for the physician's emotional life and the greatest measure of aid for the patient" (*Ibid.*).

It is clear from these remarks that Freud is concerned about the interests of both members of the psychotherapeutic dyad. This coldness of feeling, he says, provides a needful protection for the analyst's emotional life, and at the same time protects the patient from any misplaced aspirations or abuse under the guise of "therapy." Freud accordingly recommends that a psychoanalyst put aside all of his own feelings and concentrate his mind on one single purpose, that of performing the analysis as skillfully as possible. Like a surgeon, a psychoanalyst is obligated to undertake all procedures that advance treatment, notwithstanding his own feelings and prejudices and his own self-interest. He must refrain from exploiting patients to attain theoretical, research, or personal objectives. In this connection it is of interest to note that overcommitment to any theoretical position limits a psychoanalyst's effectiveness as a therapist and constitutes one of the more frequent and more pernicious sources of unanalyzed countertransference resistances.

A mature and normal adult is a person who does not suppose that others are engrossed in his personal problems and his state of well-being, but has taken onto himself the primary responsibility for his own protection and gratification. He has abandoned unrealistic expectations that the world or other people will relate to him as benevolent parents, and has shifted from an ego-centered view to a more objective view of himself and the world. He thus places his wishes into perspective with reality and minimizes projective distortions arising from wishful thinking. His mature ego is able to tolerate the frustration of knowing that he cannot always have what he wants but that he must renounce gratifications that are unattainable.

Emotionally immature individuals cling tenaciously to the ungratified wishes of their infancy and refuse to surrender these even in the face of clear evidence that wish-fulfillment has long since become a virtual impossibility. It is easy to see that such persons will continue, both in analysis and outside of it, to seek parental surrogates upon whom they will endeavor to transfer the responsibility for their personal care and happiness.

But even the mightiest are not immune from wishful thinking when the need is great enough. It will be remembered that Freud had a marked propensity to develop transference attachments and did so to a succession of heroes, among whom can be numbered Brücke ("the greatest authority I ever met"), Helmholtz ("he is one of my idols"), Meynert ("in whose footsteps I followed with such veneration"), Breuer ("he radiates light and warmth"), and later Fliess, Jung, Ferenczi, and a host of others. These attachments were usually terminated by an emotional crisis which was soon followed by a kind of reaction formation. But while the positive transference continued it was difficult for Freud to evaluate the creative productions of these men realistically. His relation to his close friend

Wilhelm Fliess is the most notable instance of this weakness. (Jones, 1953.)

Psychoanalysts since Freud have continued to develop, on account of their didactic personal analyses, transferences to their teachers. And many have in addition developed transferences to Freud and many of the other distinguished members of the profession. Just as Freud "idolized" Helmholtz from his reputation and writings alone, just so do many psychoanalysts "idolize" Freud, Jung, Adler, and others. These transferences are all the more insidious because they are unconscious and go unnoticed by the psychoanalysts who fall victim to them. This denies them an opportunity either to modify and resolve these transferences or to become aware of the effect they have upon their theoretical outlook and therapeutic approach. It is often difficult to distinguish between neurotic adhesiveness on the one hand and a rational preference for and adherence to a particular psychoanalytic school of theory and practice on the other. Freud (1915) observed: "Whoever is familiar with the nature of neurosis will not be astonished to hear that even a man who is very well able to carry out analysis upon others can behave like any other mortal and be capable of producing violent resistances as soon as he himself becomes the object of analytic investigation."

Many psychoanalysts may well wish to deny that unresolved transferences to their training analysts or to renowned figures in the field persist among the graduates of well-conducted training analyses. This may be so. But the perfect analysis is an ideal that is hardly ever realized, if it is possible at all. In fact, as we shall endeavor to show, the idea of a perfect analysis is a chimera arising from the unresolved transference itself. Edith Weigert (1952) writes, ". . . like Ferenczi, I cannot count many completed analyses in a practice of some twenty years."

Though few analysts lay claim to perfection, still they shy from the knowledge of their own imperfections. To those who can survive such a narcissistic injury, the awareness of shortcomings in their heroes, as well as the consciousness of personal shortcomings, may enable them to surrender what little comfort derives from the illusion of omnipotence in exchange for the benefit of a more objective appraisal of their abilities. We remain indebted to Ernest Jones (1953) for his careful biography of Freud, for he succeeds in making this god mortal without in any way detracting from his genius, thus releasing us forever from thralldom and the worship of this great man.

While it has become fairly easy for psychoanalysts to forgo whatever ego satisfaction there is to be derived from the uncritical overestimation of themselves by patients in the throes of transference love, they have not been so ready to renounce the narcissistic rewards they derive from the praise and respect of their colleagues. This is one of the reasons, I think, why some analysts feel compelled to cloak their work and procedures in secrecy and shy from publication. Summing up his years of observation, Martin (1956) concluded that the responses advanced by his colleagues as the reason for not making scientific contributions "served the purpose of hiding the fact that they were afraid of unfavorable criticism. To make it a requirement that one first acquire the 'omniscience' of the elders before taking the risk of expressing his own ideas is to put it succinctly—to be at the mercy of an underlying castration anxiety."

Until recently papers on countertransference, treatment failures, and errors which exposed the analyst as a person have been relatively rare. For instance, from 1952 to 1957 only four out of 135 articles that appeared in the *Psychoanalytic Quarterly* dealt with countertransference. Analysts have been exceedingly loath to be frank and explicit about what actually goes on during their treatment hours, often acting as if they were sacrosanct. This attitude has contributed more than a little to the failure of treatment techniques to keep pace with our growing understanding of human behavior. Only cross-validation, critical evaluation, and interdisciplinary cross-fertilization (virtually impossible under conditions of secrecy) can save analytic technique from stagnating into an empty ritual.

"You know that we have never been proud of the fullness and finality of our knowledge and capacity; as at the beginning, we are ready now to admit the incompleteness of our understanding, to learn new things and to alter our methods in any way that yields better results," Freud (1919) stated. Then what accounts for the unwillingness or inability on the part of analysts to be experimental or to report the results of departures from the well-known and the well-worn paths of orthodox psychoanalytic procedure? What prevents analysts from embarking upon independent research and innovation in their techniques and in their ways of looking at things? Moreover, what accounts for the resistance and hostility on the part of many analysts when such innovations are suggested or reported? Psychoanalytic theory and practice are surely still far from perfected.

These questions find a ready-made answer. Psychoanalysts who exhibit such attitudes of opposition to experiment are behaving precisely as neurotics behave. A neurosis, after all, is a compulsive form of repetition of a pattern of behavior learned in the past but which is not modified to meet the demands of the present situation. This particular form of neurosis is a peculiar one, however. It seems somehow related to a psychoanalyst's own didactic analysis and it seems to consist, in the main, of a compulsive repetition of his experience with his own analyst. Just as a patient recreates his own Oedipal relationship with an analyst, just so may an analyst recreate his own analysis with a patient. He does with his patient what his own analyst did with him. Or, he may do with his patient what he *desired* his own analyst to do with him. There is, of course, not necessarily harm in this when it is done consciously, because identification with a patient sometimes advances an analysis. But overidentification with a patient signifies that an analyst suffers from an unresolved transference neurosis related to his own analysis. Just as a healthy, mature adult ceases to overidentify with children and ceases to feel weaker than and dependent on his parents, so a mature analyst ceases to over-identify with his patients and to feel independent of and equal to his own analyst.

Weigert (1952) observed, that "the resistances of transference disappear toward the end of a successful analysis and that a greater spontaneity between analyst and analysand is established. The spontaneity of the analysand is only possible if he no longer feels compelled to please, to placate, to test, or to provoke the analyst." He must be able to relate to him as another adult and he must become capable of thinking for himself. As long as an analyst looks with awe upon his own analyst, not having been able to establish a real relationship to him, he has failed to resolve his transference, and this circumstance will eventuate in neurotic manifestations.

Besides the countertransference rule, no other rule of technique has suffered more distortion and abuse than the so-called abstinence rule that Freud described in his 1919 paper. *"Analytical treatment should be carried through, as far as it is possible, under privation— in a state of abstinence."* This has been taken to mean, in spite of Freud's explicit instruction to the contrary, that patients should be deprived of every form of gratification both in and outside of treatment. But again a more careful reading of Freud shows that this is far from the case. "By abstinence, however, is not to be understood doing without any and every satisfaction," Freud says, ". . . nor do we mean what it popularly connotes, refraining from sexual intercourse. . . . A certain amount must of course be permitted to him, more or less according to the nature of the case and the patient's individuality."

Analysts have nevertheless all too frequently used the notion that frustration is good for patients as a rationalization for abstaining from decent and compassionate behavior when such actions could be entirely justified. The issues that must bear the most intensive scrutiny are when and under what conditions gratification of a patient's needs are therapeutically indicated and when and with respect to what kind of needs gratification would merely cosset the patient's neurosis. On these issues Freud is crystal clear. The analyst, Freud says, must energetically oppose the satisfaction of *substitutive* or *neurotic* needs. An analyst out of the fullness of his heart and his readiness to help should not extend to a patient *all* of the help that one human being may wish to receive from another. It is not good to extend *too much* help. Nor should one make things *too* pleasant for a patient so that he finds satisfactions in the treatment that he might better find elsewhere. The goal of treatment is to make a patient stronger and more able to carry out the actual tasks of living. Thus the treatment should not be allowed to become a substitute for facing life.

These mandates cannot and should not be construed to mean that under no circumstances can an analyst permit himself to make things pleasant or to meet his patient's needs. In fact, quite the contrary is often the case, especially with very young or very helpless patients. Such patients by virtue of their infantile and dependent state of development bring us a whole array of *maturational* needs which are our obligation to fulfill. Indeed one of the major technical goals of treatment is gratification of maturational needs, for failure to gratify such needs inhibits the process of maturation and growth. One has to be extremely careful not to throw the baby out with the dirty bath water. Both frustration (of substitutive needs) and gratification (of maturational needs) are required. Gratification of maturational needs prepares a patient to be able to renounce substitutive gratifications.

To give force to these pronouncements I shall briefly recount my behavior with respect to two patients, Jane and Mary, both of whom can be described as extremely infantile dependent women, each of whom had at one time or another been hospitalized with acute episodes. It is not my intention to suggest that the two cases are necessarily diagnostically comparable but merely to examine the differences in my own attitude and behavior as an analyst. In Jane's case I believe I acted as a normal compassionate human being and in Mary's I did not. Jane was recently treated by me; Mary, in an earlier stage of my development. In both cases the patients developed typically intense erotic narcissistic transference attachments to me. As parents do for babies, I became for them the source of hope, love, and survival. For Mary, I was unfortunately still unprepared by temperament and training to enact this role; for Jane (perhaps thanks in part to my experience with Mary) I willingly assumed these responsibilities. The differences in the outcomes were equally dramatic.

When Mary came to me over 15 years ago and detailed the dreadful history of her life and problems I did not feel any less compassion for her than I did when I became Jane's therapist 15 years later. My trouble was that with Mary I was still encumbered by my fear of countertransference reactions and my belief in the validity of the abstinence rule. So when this unhappy and deluded young woman became financially destitute because her acute and crippling emotional state made it impossible for her to function and to support herself and to continue to pay her analytic fees, I felt obliged (against my own compassionate wishes) to discharge her from treatment. I felt that I would be pandering to her dependency and to her "unrealistic" expectations if I allowed her to continue in treatment without having to pay. The very next morning I was informed that Mary had suffered an acute psychotic episode and had been hospitalized. She had run up onto the stage in the middle of a theatrical performance, interrupting the show and begging the leading man to "Help me!"

No man can rewrite history, and perhaps it is idle to speculate on what the outcome might have been had I acted as any compassionate human being might have done in similar circumstances, but my intuition tells me that had I done so things might have ended differently for Mary.

I cannot use the case of Jane to prove this contention, because the circumstances and the personalities of the two women are so different. But I would like to report what Jane said to me to substantiate the proposition that simple compassionate behavior can sometimes alter the course of events when a patient is in acute need. When I heard that Jane had been picked up and brought to the hospital in a fugue state (due to overmedication and alcohol) and was lying alone in the psychiatric ward of a city hospital, I visited her there. I did this because I felt compassion for her and because I knew that besides me, the only creature that she cared about was her dog, who might still be locked up and unattended in her apartment. I was worried about the dog and I knew that she would be also. Jane was indeed alone and half conscious in her bed when I entered the ward. The gratitude in her eyes was quite moving to me as I bent over and exchanged a few reassuring remarks with her and discussed what I would do to provide for "Trixie."

Jane was eventually transferred to a medical ward and hovered close to death for many weeks. She slowly recovered her strength, though she remained partially paralyzed for a while, regaining the use of her arm by sheer hard work and will. The road back to physical and mental health (she will never fully attain either) took about a year but was quite notable. One day, quite spontaneously, she turned to me and remarked, "I have been meaning to tell you something for a long time. You know, you saved my life. I had lost hope and I didn't want to live any more that day in the hospital. But I opened my eyes and I saw your face. You were smiling and I knew you cared about me and that things weren't so bad. Thank you."

Appeal to authority for the justification of any procedure is anathema to science. Resistance to modifications in technique in the face of therapeutic failures is equally irrational. Unless analysts determine to be, as all scientists must, disinterested, objective and concerned about ascertaining the nature of reality rather than to be ruled by faith in their masters and the necessity to live up to tyrannical superego ideals, psychoanalysis and psychoanalytic treatment will become a sterile ritual enjoyed neither by the priests nor the acolytes.

REFERENCES

FREUD, S. The Future Prospects of Psycho-Analytic Therapy (1910), in *Collected Papers,* Vol. 2. London: Hogarth Press and Institute for Psychoanalysis, 1949.

FREUD, S. Recommendations for Physicians on the Psycho-Analytic Method of Treatment (1912). *Ibid.*

FREUD, S. Further Recommendations in the Technique of Psycho-Analysis (1913). *Ibid.*

FREUD, S. Turnings in the Ways of Psycho-Analytic Therapy (1919). *Ibid.*

FREUD, S. Analysis Terminable and Interminable (1937). *Ibid.* Vol. 5. 1950.

JONES, E. *The Life and Work of Sigmund Freud.* Vol. 1. New York: Basic Books, 1953.

MARTIN, P. W. Note on Inhibition of Scientific Productivity. *Psychoanalytic Quarterly,* 1956, 25:415–417.

WEIGERT, E. Contribution to the Problem of Terminating Psychoanalysis. *Psychoanalytic Quarterly,* 1952, 21:465–480.

How Not to Succeed in Psychotherapy

EARL G. WITENBERG, M. D.

THERE IS ample evidence that psychotherapy is an impossible profession. The structure of both the training and treatment situations lends itself to ambiguity, rationalization, and dogmatism. As Lawrence Kubie has said, our data come from "fallible reports of fallible recollections of fallible perceptions of a swift and irrecoverable series of complicated events, in which the observers themselves were emotionally involved" (Kubie, 1968). Attempts to correct this by use of direct observation and direct experience (such as the video tape recorder, the audio tape recorder, and the one-way viewing room) add knowledge but introduce new factors which color the field and alter the process.

THE ANALYST'S ROLE

Notwithstanding the difficulties of communication inherent to the process, we have a model for the psychoanalyst. He should be one who accepts and tries to understand the most private communications, verbal and nonverbal, of another person. He must be able to maintain an atmosphere in which (unlike any other situation) everything is permitted; where the other person is encouraged to say whatever comes to mind whether it is relevant or not, whether it is affiliative or disjunctive. Such a structure sets the stage for the appearance of regressive phenomena which the analyst must notice and interpret with the patient. Furthermore, the analyst must realize that the need for relatedness exists in all people; he must also acknowledge that *syntaxic communication* is possible between any of them whether they are a butcher and a poet, a saint and a sinner, a judge and a criminal. This communication is reciprocal and should be transformative so that the impact of one person on another results in change.

It has been demonstrated that the very survival of infants depends on the nature of the mothering process; this fact proves the importance of relatedness.

Each of us forms whatever relationship he can in a given situation; the treatment situation is designed to facilitate, utilize, and make explicit the kinds of relationships that arise. The therapeutic relationship is not only a causal relationship, it is also a logical relationship. The therapist must see the patient as a different way of stating what he, the therapist, is himself. He must recognize that the patient and the therapist alike possess a potential for a variety of human experiences; thus the hopes, wishes, fears, and anxieties which dwell in one of them may exist, at any time, in the other. The therapist must be "abstinent" in the relationship; that is, he must monitor any change in himself so that he does not introduce his own needs or anxieties into the psychotherapeutic situation. He must distinguish the real from the unreal in what the patient says about him. He must be aware that the patient's intense experience with him is only a step toward the achievement of the goals on which they have agreed, and that this interchange takes place in a context that is contrived-acceptance-no-matter-what, regular-fixed hours, fee-for-time, and it is therefore not directly translatable into a social situation.

How can one ever succeed in being this firm, kind, curious, abstinent, accepting, understanding, and undemanding expert? The answer is that this is possible only sometimes with all people and all the time with no one. The most critical task for the therapist is to recognize the immediate and ongoing impact of the therapeutic situation and its relationship to future goals.

Whenever an analyst steps out of the analytic role, either emotionally or actually, he has failed his patient. It is the function of the analyst to be with the patient emotionally and yet to be free of any anxieties regarding this emotion. The analyst must be curious and courageous. He must be able to understand the patient, both cognitively and conatively, by identifying with the patient, by putting himself in the patient's place and then placing what he feels, senses, and experiences into a cognitive framework. This shifting back and forth between the feeling level and the cognitive level is the essence of the analyst's task. The psychoanalyst must be able to inquire as to what is unclear and therefore must be prepared to expose his own ignorance. He must be able to experience the unspoken, unconscious wishes and fears of his patients without being intimidated by them. He must know what emotions are evoked in him and must be ready to see how they apply or do not apply to the particular person in the particular therapeutic setting with particular goals in mind.

Exposing himself to the levels of intricate emotion and anxiety of another person, the analyst must understand what part of his response is evoked by the other one's wishes, fears, and demands and what part is evoked by his own unresolved wishes, fears, and demands. This understanding keeps him from using the patient for his own needs; it also enables him to know what the patient is actually doing. The analyst must be able to participate with the patient, to observe him, and to blend both of these activities appropriately. Learning technique, the how-to-do-this, is comparatively simple, once the therapist is clear as to how and what is being communicated.

THE PITFALLS

Treatment is heuristically divided into a beginning, a middle, and a terminal phase. There are pitfalls specific to each of these phases. The nature of the errors will depend upon the personality and experience of the therapist and of the patient, and the relationship between them.

The Beginning Phase

In *the beginning phase of treatment,* the presenting complaint and the detailed anamnesis are reviewed and evaluated. Hopefully a working alliance is established. Unless there is agreement about the specific reasons and goals for the recurring meetings, treatment will founder and perhaps fail. In some instances patients come only so that they may have a human relationship. In other words, they'd like some company. These people are not suitable for treatment, which is, after all, an aid to living and not a substitute for life. Failure to ascertain the goals of the patient or to state the implications of the patient's dilemma results in a confused picture. This is illustrated by the following example:

Some years ago I received a telephone call from a physician who asked me to see a patient of his, Mrs. X, who for two years had been complaining of gastrointestinal symptoms which had not responded to tranquilizers or other treatment. I agreed to see the patient and several days later this nicely dressed, composed woman came to my office and proceeded to describe her symptoms. I asked her about her marriage; this subject occupied us till the end of the session, at which point I said to her, "You have told me that your husband has physically beaten you to the extent where you have required medical attention on several occasions. You have told me that through devious means he is taking your inheritance away from you. You have told me that for the last two years, concurrent with the onset of your symptoms, he has quite openly been playing around with a good friend of yours. There must be some deep reason that you remain in this relationship. I think it would pay us to find out about that." We made another appointment. Twenty-four hours later she called me to say that her symptoms were gone and that "thank you very much" she did not need another appointment. Three weeks later I received a telephone call from an attorney who reported that Mrs. X was seated in his office having just informed him that I had advised a divorce for reasons of her health.

Failure on my part to ascertain her conscious goals, or to make explicit to her that the same characteristics which accounted for her present life situation would lead her to a similar dilemma without therapy, obviated a chance for resolution of her personal difficulty —divorce or no divorce.

The sequel to Mrs. X's case is of considerable interest. Mr. X married his mistress, who, as the second Mrs. X, developed gastrointestinal symptoms for which she sought relief from the same physician who had treated the first Mrs. X. Again I received a phone call from this doctor, who, in something of an understatement, suggested that I might like to see the second wife. Into my office walked the second Mrs. X; the similarity to her predecessor in appearance, attire, and symptomatology was striking. She told essentially the same story as the first Mrs. X, echoing that lady's acceptance of the treatment. Her husband had beaten her. He was sexually involved with a friend of hers. And while he had not misappropriated an inheritance (there being none), he had somehow misused monies intended for her children from her first marriage. At the end of the session I asked her what was her goal. It was to get rid of the symptoms. When I pointed out to her that maybe she had more basic issues to grapple with, namely, what had induced her to become involved with a man whose conduct was known to her, she accepted the idea of treatment, after two more hours of consultation, with a revised concept of her goals. Referral was then made of a symptom-free but motivated person.

In attempting to establish a working alliance with his patient, the analyst must be aware that any of his traits, appropriate or less so, may be used by the patient to increase resistance and impede progress. A useful trait in an analyst, such as his interest in learning about others and about himself, can increase resistance and make underlying pathology obvious. The following case illustrates this point.

A man came to me at the suggestion of his analyst for consultation. I had referred him originally to this analyst two years prior. I asked what had brought him back. He said it was to tell me off for having made a "bum referral." His documentation of his charges was vague and indeterminate. He asked if he should continue treatment. I replied, "I don't know what therapy has to offer you. You had three years with Dr. A and have just completed two years with Dr. B. You know what it is all about. You tell me how one sat like a Buddha and went over all the symbols in dreams with you; how the other took an active interest in you. None of it seemed to work." He asked if we could meet to try to make some sense of it. I could not offer him a regular hour but agreed to see him whenever possible. "If you want to come, we can figure out what you are coming for," I said.

He came. I was at first aloof, polite, formal, curious,

and challenging. One day he had a dream which he interpreted in a way that was very significant for him. I became interested, somewhat excited in this discovery, as is my style. The feeling that I was succeeding where others had failed did little to allay my enthusiasm. The next day he came in and said, "I am depressed. I am lonely. I have no one, no one likes me. Analysis doesn't work," and so forth. The work of the previous day had lost meaning. Interest and engagement had been replaced by depression and withdrawal. We explored the reason for his altered attitude and change in mood. At first he saw no reason—just the way he was; he couldn't use understanding or insight, he was in the wrong field, he loved no one, if only he could find the right girl.

I asked if he had noticed anything different about the previous session. He eventually focused on my interest in him, which he said was stimulated by his performance and maintained that prior to that I had had no personal stake in how he did. My inquiry as to what the entire sequence meant to him brought a flood of associations regarding people who "took an interest" in him. He then went on to relate his feelings about his "over-interested fat father," telling how he would inveigle his father into discussions on professional problems and then disappoint or get angry with his father. The central difficulty in the therapy, as in life, had become any hint of a narcissistic interest that another person (in this case the analyst) might have had in the patient.

No analyst can enter a working relationship with a

patient without gaining something for himself. What is necessary is that the analyst realize that any trait of his (even ones with which he is pleased) may adversely influence the therapy and that he be aware of these traits and understand their impact on the other person. In this instance love of one's work and its accomplishments evoked a response in a patient which has taken many sessions to clarify and is not yet resolved.

The Middle Phase

The *middle phase of treatment* is concerned with accumulating data about the causes and sources of dissociation or repression. During this phase, one makes explicit significant transferential operations. The most common pitfall is to settle for information rather than making the process explicit. For example, the analyst confronted by a patient who says "I cannot tell you about some feeling I had about you," or "I cannot tell you about some details in the dream I had, "should fix his attention on the patient's inability to tell, which is more important than that which is not being told. Very often the patient is able to reveal what he is concealing; he finds it more difficult to tell his reasons for not telling. The therapist who settles for content is failing his patient. Significant information about the relationship, in some cases transferential, in others real, is being inattended by both. By falling into the "patient's trap" and accepting "secrets" as a peace offering, the therapist increases resistance and prolongs treatment.

The Need to Be Helpful

The need to be helpful (omnipotent?) is another trait that often boomerangs on the therapist. Quite frequently this is verbalized as, "After all, I'm a physician," or "As his doctor, I felt it was important to be available." Action based on this attitude often impedes the patient's ability to see his dependency strivings as unrealistic. The "doctor" blindly utilizing this defense tacitly legitimizes and increases the dependency strivings. To the patient this attitude makes the demands realistic. The double-edged nature of such an attitude is evidenced in two illustrations.

In 1947 a 30-year-old World War II veteran came to see me complaining of total sexual impotence of four months' duration. He had been married for three of the four months. Prior to that time, since the age of 17, he had been sexually effective with his wife and with other women. He had never completed high school and was working as a skilled laborer. He had had intense war experience as a bombardier (he had flown 20 missions) and as a P.O.W. (he had escaped from a prison camp and had hidden in Italy for six months, protected by partisans). I saw this man once a week for 26 weeks. By the end of this period he had regained his potency and was earning his high school diploma by completing a series of equivalency exams.

Over the years, this man has called for appointments on approximately eight occasions spaced by two- to three-year intervals, for a total of approximately 30 additional hours. He has remarried and has a good relationship with his wife, he has completed his college education and earned a graduate degree, and finally he has become a professional man whose ability has been rewarded by continuous promotions within a leading organization in which he will very shortly become partner. His brief returns to therapy have always been occasioned by anxiety about a promotion, a raise, or a change in status. At these times he would call me and I would eagerly make myself available to him within 48 hours. We examined his need to defeat himself by frustrating what, he believed, were his boss's aspirations for him, but unwittingly encouraged this very same behavior in the analytic relationship. To "help" this patient by always being there for him in an accepting and unchallenging environment was to support his dependency and court his hostility, both of which have contributed to his persistent effort to prove wrong those who expressed faith in him. The irrational aspects of his dependency have never become clear to him. In retrospect I would have been more therapeutic had I been less of a "doctor."

Only a few data are available to me about the patient whose therapy provides the second illustration. The contact was with the analyst who came to me because of his distress following the patient's suicide. This analyst is eminently competent and likes to think of himself as a dedicated "doctor," always available. Five years ago the patient had terminated a successful three-year treatment. She had found happiness in her marriage, her family, and her work. She seemingly had resolved her mourning for a mother who had committed suicide 10 years previously. The patient's success was particularly gratifying to her analyst, whose need to be helpful increased the significance of her/their achievement, and who used the treatment experience as teaching material.

When the patient called to return to treatment, the analyst felt disappointed and mildly annoyed, yet eager to see her. When during the sessions the patient communicated a sense of increasing anxiety, urgency, and futility, the analyst placed her on ataractic and anti-depressant medication while he attempted in the last days of their contact to impress her with the validity of their mutual understanding. While both her husband and her analyst were out of town, the patient killed herself.

It is impossible to say what might have obviated this outcome, but it is clear that the analyst's need to be helpful made it too difficult for the factors of irrational dependency and consequent rage to be resolved. By attempting to be helpful, the therapist made himself helpless in the face of the irrational demands of the patient, who could not fully express her wishes or see their irrationality. The need "to take charge of the patient," "to be the doctor" alters the structure of the relationship. One of the untoward results is that the patient is unable to see his or her demands as being unrealistic or irrational. The analyst makes himself available to the patient as a dedicated, respectful expert who is inquiring as to the patient's emotional life, but when he oversteps his role and "takes care of" the patient, he himself distorts the therapeutic relationship.

The Terminal Phase

Much has been written about the *terminal phase* of *therapy*. The hazards of this stage originate in the fear generated in both therapist and patient by every patient's final resting place—the extraordinary challenge of real-life situations. It is here that one does well to remember that the main question in therapy is: Has the goal been achieved? If not, can it be? One has to be clear about what has been accomplished in the treatment.

There are any number of methods (and as many "reasons") to impede the effectiveness of this final stage of therapy. A therapist may prolong this stage indefinitely by continually hitting upon gray areas which still "need working on." Because of the structure of the relationship and particularly because of fear of separation, the patient often goes along with this. Sometimes the patient will properly deny the validity of the analyst's assertion that other problems "need working on." The analyst's response at this point may be of such a nature that the patient can leave only by denying his anxiety about leaving, and he leaves, so to speak, in a counter-phobic manner.

A therapist may resist termination initiated by the patient for a good reason such as transfer of job or going away to college. The therapist shows his resistance by labeling the termination "premature" and suggesting treatment is not "finished." Implicit here is the therapist's anxiety about separation, his notion that therapy has a definite time limit, and that less time means lesser results, as if to say that the efforts and accomplishments of a short time have no merit unless one gets a diploma for the course. By maintaining a neutral attitude and accepting the reality of the external exigencies (let's see what we can do in this period of time), the therapist can avail himself of the opportunity to see that patients can be exceedingly productive under externally set time limits. The therapist has to learn to cope with the anxiety of letting someone grow up at his own rate, as well as handling his own anxiety about separation from the patient.

A number of patients announce their readiness to leave by reviving their original symptoms, long since gone. This revival is a *disguise for separation anxiety* and it is, covertly, a test of the therapist's willingness to let them go. Making explicit the separation anxiety as well as the fear of leaving resolves this issue. No patient should leave treatment without a mutual recounting of the issues covered, the goals achieved or failed, the delineation of the varying nature of the relationship, both real and unreal. The discoveries of positives as well as the uncovering of negatives have to be spelled out.

How to Structure the Therapeutic Situation

In the above, traditional caveats have been shunned. Much has been written about them. From the moment of the first phone call to the last goodbye, psychotherapy is fraught with opportunities for error. The assumption that psychotherapy or psychoanalysis

is a process into which all people fit is a frequent cause
of failure; the identical approach to different patients
often results in failure; also the belief that the therapeutic goals can be identical for all dooms effective
treatment. The recommendation of uniform frequency
and visits stereotypes an individualized procedure and
dehumanizes its effectiveness. The proper blend of respect, concern, interest, objectivity, activity, and recep-
tivity varies from individual to individual and from
session to session and will determine the course. The
teaching and the learning have to take place in individualized doses. The focus here has been on some of the
dilemmas faced by the analyst: How to structure the
therapeutic situation; how the personality (character
structure, wishes, fears, and anxieties) of the analyst increases the difficulty of treatment. Can the analyst's
personality offer an opportunity for greater clarity if he
himself is aware of these factors and their impact on
the patient's perception of reality?

In summary, the journey we call psychotherapy is
taken by two people: one an expert in living and its vicissitudes, the other with problems in living. The journey has a definite beginning marked by mutual agreement as to the specific reasons for starting. After the
initial reconnaissance, there is sharing of intended
goals. There is a long, intensive period of spelling out
the details of living which have made the person what
he is. Once there is sufficient clarity and the person
knows himself to the same extent as his analyst knows
him, the time for separation has come. The pitfalls on

this journey are far too many to be enumerated. At any time when the therapist loses sight of the fact that there is a discrete beginning and a definite ending, psychotherapy may end in failure. *Therapy cannot be a substitute for life, for either the therapist or his patient.* The therapeutic situation is so structured that it requires constant vigilance on the part of the therapist to make certain that whatever regression takes place it is always in the service of treatment. Success or failure depends on how the therapist uses his transferences, countertransferences, and his *real self* in the treatment situation. Within this relationship change will take place and with proper alertness transformation will occur.

REFERENCES

KUBIE, L. S. A Review of Jay Haley (ed.). Advanced techniques of Hypnosis and Therapy: Selected Papers of Milton H. Erikson. *The Journal of Nervous and Mental Disease,* 1968, **3**: 147.

My Failures: Some of Them and How They Grew

EDWARD J. HORNICK, M.D.

INTRODUCTION

THERE ARE two ways of achieving a failure in psychotherapy or psychoanalysis. The preferred and safest way is not to try anything. The apathetic, indifferent, stony-faced therapist cannot be blamed for intruding into the patient's thoughts or life. He need not risk a continuous testing of his own hypotheses about the dynamics of mental disorder, nor need he gamble his own feelings in relation to the patient. That nothing happens in treatment, or that the patient responds with occasional rage, can be attributed to the therapist only as a sin by *omission* on his part. However, such an accusation can be easily dismissed by any "thoughtful" therapist as a sign of impatience by the patient; this impatience must be met firmly by the therapist with more indifference. In this fashion, a full-fledged therapeutic failure can be explained as a proof of serious illness of the patient, and the therapist's responsibility is thus discounted.

On the other hand, the therapist or analyst who does take an active part in the conduct of the treatment runs the more serious risk of a sin by *commission*. The active position makes him liable to censure by the patient, by the patient's family, by his peers, or by himself. By exposing himself, the psychoanalyst has muddied the waters of transference; he has possibly injured the delicate skin of the patient's psyche, and he may be involving himself in a countertransferential acting out. He certainly may be wrong in his evaluation of the problem and in his action in relation to that evaluation. As a physician, he has violated the first rule of medicine, *primum non nocere* (the first duty of the doctor is not to harm the patient). With therapists in other professions that stricture may be less inhibiting, and hence active intervention more attractive. The therapeutic activist, wherever he comes from, makes himself visible and vulnerable, and serves as an easy target for the failed patient and his social group.

The comparison of the two types of psychotherapy exposes the writer's strong preference for a failure that results from a conscientious sin of commission rather than a failure by the sin of omission.

THREE FRAMING PROPOSITIONS ABOUT FAILURE

(1). It is true that therapeutic failure may have some relation to a misguided plan or execution of therapy. However, in psychotherapy one must always explore the possibility that the unconscious of the therapist is for its own reasons working *against* success of the treatment. Thus whenever treatment is going badly an immediate self-analysis of the therapist is imperative. Dr. Harold Searles, in his paper, The Effort to Drive the Other Person Crazy—An Element in the

Aetiology and Psychotherapy of Schizophrenia, demonstrated how effectively therapists can keep their patients sick because they know the specific triggers to touch.

(2). The second framing proposition is that we know very little about the definition of illness and cure. It is somehow simpler when the symptoms are unpleasant or painful to the patient; however, more often today we are involved in treating characterological traits which are closely related to varying definitions of what the good life is supposed to be. When the therapist defines cure as the patient's arrival at the therapist's *weltanschauung,* then the therapist is possibly dealing with philosophy rather than with psychotherapy. The difference in style and goals between therapists and their patients has become most apparent in regard to middle-class therapists and their lower-class patients.

This is but a broad example. In every therapeutic relationship disparate views between therapist and patient are bound to appear. They disagree on such issues as what is *really* wrong, what needs to be done, eventually also about what has been accomplished. Many of the failures in treatment originate in differences in life-style which have gone unrecognized.

(3). A third painful approach to the study of failure involves a critical survey of the practice of practice, including such issues as fee-setting. It seems that the entire arrangement of doing psychoanalysis or psychotherapy is artificial and procrustean—Procrustes was the innkeeper outside Athens who stretched or chopped his guests to fit his bed. The therapeutic bed may be 40 minutes or 45 minutes or 50 minutes long; it may be available to clients once a week or six times a week. It may be unusable for one or two months in the summer or a week or two in the winter. Whatever the conditions they are set by the therapist, and the patient must lie on the bed or the couch as dictated by the therapist. Whether the patient lies down or sits up or has some choice in the matter, how the fee is set and collected, all these conditions represent technical features of the treatment which sometimes grossly, and sometimes subtly, bear on the cure of the patient.

TWO EXAMPLES OF FAILURE

Willa

Willa was 34 when she was initially seen in consultation in New York City. She had just come to the city from the midwest, where she had been in psychotherapy for two years. She had initiated treatment after a brief hospitalization for severe anxiety when she witnessed a slasher stabbing women in Chicago. When initially seen in New York, Willa reported an inability to sleep more than two or three hours a night; weight fluctuation of 20–25 pounds; phobias of airplanes, small animals, and heights; hypochondriasis; and depression. Her father had hanged himself five years before. She felt herself to be somewhat responsible since she had refused to have him forcibly hospitalized. She was seen once weekly in supportive psychotherapy and has improved. However, her symptoms never abated sufficiently to warrant discharge, and she was still coming for treatment in February 1962.

At that time I lost patience. She was in simultaneous individual and group treatment, which I had recommended for increased socialization. She was quarreling with both me and the group leader and playing us off against each other, while refusing to do anything constructive for herself. It was suggested that she become an assistant leader in the group, a role she declined because she didn't want to be like her mother. As her individual therapist I decided that the time had come after six years to take a strong line with her. I told her that she was not getting anywhere in treatment or in life, hoping that my admonition would persuade her to shape up and ship out.

A week later, she confessed to all sorts of vengeful notions of blowing up my house, cutting off my penis, and committing suicide. However, she said at the same time that I was trying to pull her down out of her cloud-cuckooland and enable her to live more effectively on earth.

During the next week she telephoned, which was unusual for her, to ask if her throat was going to split down the middle. I recognized this as a psychotic fear, but thinking that the boat might have to weather a squall to get to port, I reassured her that her throat would be all right. It later became clear that her throat and my throat were the same and she thought I was talking out of both sides of my throat. Two days later, she phoned again to say that she had just wired President John F. Kennedy to inform him that the atomic bomb was about to drop on New York. She called me only because she was having trouble getting through to J. F. K.

I suggested that she come over immediately, which she did. She arrived by taxicab; she happened to have 50 dollars in her pocketbook, which she gave to a very surprised and grateful cabbie. Obviously money was of no use once the world was to be blown up. My patient was and is a very elegant and polite, gentle woman who always maintained a considerable reserve in the office. On this occasion, she entered and sat at my feet like a little child and started to tell me about this horrible thing that was going to happen which she had gleaned through clairvoyance. She maintained that she was the Virgin Mary and that I was Jesus Christ. She told me that she was pregnant, having been impregnated by my words of wisdom. She also told me that I was insane. She said that she was homosexual and so was I, and that was why she could not do anything more physical. She wanted to save both me and my family from destruction. She had already telephoned her own mother to see whether she had survived.

I realized that I had literally driven her crazy. I had driven her crazy because we were symbiotically tied to each other. By throwing a wedge between us and by bawling her out so vigorously I had broken that tie much too rapidly, much too painfully, and much too harmfully. Hence, she went crazy. I apologized to her in the most sincere way I could muster, and she gave up her psychosis on the spot. She seated herself in her customary chair opposite me and apologized to me for going crazy. At the present time she is still in once-a-week psychotherapy, still not totally improved but she has not been crazy again.

Mark

Mark was an eighteen-year-old, talented, schizophrenic boy who had been hospitalized for two years in a private sanitarium. The doctors in the sanitarium felt that it was unsafe for him to be at large. Mark loved his motorcycle, which he drove skillfully but somewhat recklessly. He was talented in writing and wished to return to regular school in order to get to college. I saw him in a consultation in May, after he had run away from the hospital. I felt that the danger of releasing him was real but that the risk had to be taken if Mark was to make some adjustment to living in society. He and I entered three-times-a-week therapeutic encounters, and his life began to make sense. Six weeks later, in mid-June, he pushed for my permission to go to Europe on a motorcycle trip with friends. I pointed out that I myself would be leaving in two more weeks for an extended holiday, but he convinced me that he would be doing his "thing," most happily and most effectively. I learned after the summer that he had taken an overdose of heroin in North Africa which killed him.

SUMMARY

Some additional data are required to understand the countertransference of the therapist in these two cases. The review of the session in which I had gotten rough with Willa, the elegant lady, revealed the following dream. "A large man was wandering around with his cock cut in half. He was holding the dead half in his hand, giving pleasure where he might to other ladies, but he was sticking the bloody end into me and it hurt." In retrospect it seems plain that the threat of castration coupled with the therapist's annoyance at her slow progress had something to do with the therapist driving her crazy.

In the case of Mark, I neglected to mention that the hospital doctors who recommended keeping Mark in a closed ward were rivals of mine in the adolescent field, and that I eagerly wished to prove them wrong and to rescue Mark from their clutches. My eagerness to move Mark led to his undoing.

A comparison between a cure for Willa and a cure for Mark is worth study. Given Willa's limited ego strength, a reasonable goal of cure for her would be a lifelong symbiosis with a therapist. Indeed, she is still in treatment, fourteen years after being seen initially. I anticipate that she will continue coming to my office as long as we both shall live. I hope to do this without feeling that I am a failure because she has not gotten well and without feeling that she is a failure as a human being because she needs me.

With Mark, the appropriate "cure" would have been to protect him through the acting-out period of his late adolescence. My failure to grasp the dimension of "cure" in both cases was a meaningful factor in both cases.

Our third framing proposition had to do with the

practice of practice. My practical expectations that Willa should get well in a limited number of years were clearly an illusion, and my practice now includes not one but several patients with whom I expect to have lifelong communication.

Mark's case illustrates, at the level of practice, how dangerous it is to take on a sick patient so soon before vacation. It is clearly impossible to know whether Mark did commit suicide, but that is a possible assumption.

An effort has been made in this paper to study two therapeutic failures in terms of the therapist's countertransference, his definition of cure for each patient, and a critique of his way of practicing psychotherapy. It seemed that all these facts were relevant to the failures which occurred.

Some Unsolved Problems of Psychoanalytic Psychotherapy

L AWRENCE S. K UBIE , M.D.

I N   THE   formulation of questions, as in the formulation of hypotheses, we must constantly keep in mind
the difference between describing the goals of psychotherapy and the techniques for reaching these
goals. No psychologist, no psychiatrist, and no psychoanalyst is immune to this confusion. Words themselves are its source. A striking example is Freud's
basic thesis concerning the goal of analytic psychotherapy, as "making the unconscious conscious"; or as
"Where the Id was, there must the Ego be. . . ."
These are closely related yet not identical characteriza-
tions of an intermediate step in therapy. Neither describes a method. Neither tells how to take this step.
Yet both are referred to as though they were technical
devices. In part this is because the description of any
goal carries implications for technique. For instance,
Freud's description implies that in analytic therapy the
transition from neurosis to normality depends upon
insight and ego functions. This, in turn, confronts us
with every unsolved problem which clusters around

Reprinted with permission from: pp. 87–102, PROGRESS IN
PSYCHOTHERAPY, 1956, Fromm-Reichmann, F., and Moreno,
J. L. (eds.); Grune & Stratton, New York, pp. 352.

the interrelated concepts of insight, resistance, transference and countertransference, catharsis and communication across the iron curtain between the conscious
and the preconscious, on the one hand, and the unconscious, on the other.

Before plunging into a discussion of the technical
difficulties which are inherent in comparisons of psychotherapies let us bear in mind one bias which can be
avoided, which in the past has invalidated most such
studies. This has been the tendency to use comparative
evaluations of the *results of psychotherapy* as occasions
for special pleading, either for or against any psychotherapy at all, by those who either oppose or prefer
an organic approach; or else comparative evaluations
have been used as a basis for special pleading for some
particular system of psychotherapy. Such biases, while
always dangerous, need not necessarily lead us astray if
they are frankly acknowledged, and if precise objective
criteria are applied for all of the methods used and for
all of the claimed results. This has not been done.

Apart from bias, however, and for reasons which I
shall describe, it is scientifically premature at this time
to attempt to compare the results of different psychotherapies, or the results of psychotherapy, with the results of no treatment at all or of treatment by the organic therapies. This statement is not a covert effort to
hide failures. I have participated in many panels, in
which I have repeatedly argued that our failures
should be studied in the spirit in which medicine has
always gone to the autopsy table; and that it is primarily out of the study of its failures that psychotherapy

can hope to achieve scientific stature, and not from the study of its successes alone, important though these are as well (Kubie, 1947). The fact remains, however, that comparisons of successes and failures in this field cannot yield accurate and dependable data until we solve the many organizational, administrative, and technical difficulties which are prerequisite. Furthermore, although such comparisons will ultimately be of great social, human, practical, and scientific importance, to attempt them prematurely will only confuse and obscure our judgment. What, then, are these difficulties?

STRATEGY OF THE PREPARATION
FOR THERAPY
Variables

As one attempts such a study one might set out to compare the psychotherapeutic results achieved in the same illness or in different illnesses either by the same therapist using one technique or by different therapists using one technique, or by the same or different therapists using different techniques. One will note at once how many variables these alternatives introduce. These are the variables which are due to such factors as the age, sex, race, accent, appearance, size, voice, hair, manner, etc., of the therapist. There are also the subtler internal idiosyncracies of the individual therapist, and the uncertain role which these play. Furthermore, the words "same or different illness," "same or different techniques" force us to ask ourselves whether we are able as yet to characterize any two illnesses as either identical or antipodal with respect to one or several features; or whether we are able to characterize two techniques as identical or different. Later, I shall attempt to explain why I do not believe that either characterization is possible at present. It is possible only to indicate the direction in which we will have to gain greater knowledge if we are to characterize psychopathologic processes and psychotherapeutic procedures with precision. Certainly until we can make such basic identifications and distinctions we will not be ready to compare the outcome of the same or of different techniques on the same or different illnesses; nor even to compare the state of patients who have received treatment with those who remained untreated.

Reluctance to Study Failures

It would be natural to assume that the most direct opportunity to study failure would be in the ordinary course of the private psychoanalytic practice of senior analysts. Certainly seniority brings the opportunity to review both our own failures and those of our colleagues. Unfortunately, however, this opportunity is limited by several facts.

With occasional exceptions the partial failures of analysis tend to draw away not only from the original analyst but from any contact with psychiatry. (This is equally true of the partial failures of other psychotherapies.) Many such ex-patients remain in a halfway state between health and illness, not suffering enough to seek further help, yet not fully well—discouraged, financially depleted, and not infrequently resentful. Families, friends, and general physicians see such ex-patients constantly, but the analyst only rarely has an opportunity to study them. The exceptions to this constitute a self-selected and atypical group. Moreover, on those rare occasions when such patients return we can hardly pretend to ourselves that we can render wholly unbiased appraisals of the reasons for our failures. (The Central Fact-Gathering Agency of the American Psychoanalytic Association is considering the many technical *difficulties of collecting statistical data* on such experiences, and their varied fates; but this essential work is just beginning.)

A senior analyst will also have opportunities occasionally to observe what happens to patients with whom he himself has failed, and whom he has referred to some other colleague. Even when the *referral* has not succeeded such patients are more grateful than the first group because they usually recognize the honesty of the referral. At some later time, therefore, they may return to the first analyst to talk it over. This provides an opportunity to study both the successes and failures of such referrals. But these opportunities also occur rarely, and constitute in some respects a weighted rather than a representative sample.

A third opportunity for the study of failures comes whenever a patient is referred by a colleague who has run up against a stone wall. I have been consulted by such "failures" of experienced colleagues from every school of psychoanalysis and psychotherapy. Yet by their very nature such referrals give us only half the picture. Unless an analyst dies or moves away before an analysis is completed, his successfully treated patients have no occasion to turn elsewhere for further help. Consequently, there are few opportunities to compare the successes of our colleagues with their failures.

Yet, in spite of all these limiting factors, if we bear them constantly in mind and if our relationships with our colleagues are sound and generous such *cross-referrals* of one another's failures could provide much more valuable data than they do at present, even if such cross-referrals under conditions of private office practice or private hospital practice can never provide a true sample.

Unfortunately, full advantage is rarely taken even of such opportunities as do arise. Analysts do not confer freely about their failures. Sometimes this is because these occasions are seized upon as opportunities to gloat over one another's failures. Sometimes it is because of the defensiveness of the discouraged analyst, who has had to acknowledge defeat after years of heartbreaking effort. Sometimes it is due to the complicated astigmatism which invades the *countertransference* during prolonged and unsuccessful struggles with difficult cases. Sometimes, on the other hand, it is the new analyst who holds aloof, fearing that any conference with a previous therapist may jeopardize his recent and highly vulnerable therapeutic rapport. On top of these considerations is the hard fact that every therapist is pressed for time.

Comparable difficulties arise in *the relation of intra-*

mural to extramural psychiatric practice. For all of these reasons, it is worth considering whether a frank discussion of these intradisciplinary relationships and an exploratory discussion of the many unique problems which surround consultations should not be given top priority.

In private practice a further source of difficulty has been the fact that *follow-up studies* of private patients present both practical and psychologic problems. Of the latter, the most obvious is the fact that such follow-ups tend to interfere with that very emancipation from dependency which is one of the goals of psychotherapy.

Need for Changes in Organization of Private Analytic Practice

These, then, are a few of the obstacles which hamper our efforts to learn from our daily experience, by making it difficult to take advantage of the opportunity to study the failures of private psychoanalytic practice. Some way of overcoming these obstacles must be found. Indeed, one of the conclusions which this review of these difficulties forces upon me is that the needs of research in psychotherapy can be served only if radical changes are made in the organization of private analytic practice and its integration with the neurosis treatment center and the psychiatric hospital. Moreover, special research institutes in psychotherapy will have obvious strategic advantages over both the private practitioner and the hospital in a study of any form of psychotherapy.

Prerequisite to Objective Studies of Psychotherapeutic Results

Differentiation Among Variables

Since we cannot split a human being down the middle and treat one half of him in one way and the other half in another, it is essential to be sure that in different human beings the responses of essentially identical psychopathologic processes are being compared. Setting up an arbitrary and unanalyzed "control" is wholly misleading. Instead, we must identify, isolate, and estimate the concurrent influence of several interdependent groups of forces in each individual: (1) the total life situation; (2) the personality (i.e., the psychopathologic soil) out of which illness grows; (3) the neurotic process itself; (4) the psychotherapeutic maneuver, including, of course, the concurrent interplay between the patient and the therapist. All analytic data must be cross-checked, corrected, and confirmed by precise investigations of the family background, early history, and social situation. Yet, it is doubtful that, in private practice, psychiatric social workers, cultural anthropologists, and clinical psychologists can coordinate their work with that of the analysts. Here again the *need for special institutes for basic research in psychoanalytic psychiatry* becomes clear.

Especially do we lack precision in our thinking about those elements in the neurotic process which run as a common thread through all of its varied manifestations, as distinct from those elements which are peculiar to each special form. It is here that the conceptual and theoretic structure of psychoanalysis is weakest, specifically because the libido theory and Freud's economic hypothesis brought to this issue a group of *a priori* assumptions which begged the basic questions. These now demand reexamination in the light of newer concepts of brain physiology (Kubie, 1947, 1954).

The differentiation between the elements in the neurotic process which are common to all and those which are special to particular syndromes must start with a differentiation between the primary steps in the neurotic process, the inevitable secondary symptomatic developments, and, in turn, their highly varied tertiary consequences. The particular form which the symptomatic neurosis assumes may result from accidental and minor events or stresses; yet the consequences of these secondary differences may constitute the most dramatic and extreme contrasts in human life.

Thus, the entire life of an individual with a masked claustrophobia—who wants to be a writer, yet cannot remain in a room long enough to set pen to paper— will differ in almost every detail from that of another individual with an identical claustrophobia who is a traveling salesman. The former will be chronically tense, restless, anxious, frustrated, and depressed. The second will be expansive and even exuberantly confident, reacting to every threat with increased activity.

The germinal mechanism of the neurosis in these two individuals may be identical; but accidental secondary forces have made the price which each pays for his neurosis and the affective state which accompanies it as different as day from night. And as a further consequence the total problem which must be resolved by psychotherapy is wholly different, in spite of the *identity of the underlying initiating mechanisms.*

Similarly, a patient with compulsive orderliness seems to be a wholly different human being from one who is equally compulsive in his disorderliness. The compulsive miser and the compulsive spendthrift, the compulsive conformist and the compulsive rebel, are twins, yet hardly seem to be related to each other. The social and personal consequences of compulsive benevolence are quite different from those of obligatory delinquency. The compulsively driven student leads a different life from that of the student with an obsessional work block. In each instance two violently contrasting symptom groups may arise from a common trunk, from which they differentiate as a result of minor and almost accidental differences. The initial dynamics of illness may be identical even in widely contrasting lives; yet their *divergent secondary consequences* accumulate through the years until human pictures which emerge at the end could hardly seem more unlike, with widely varied consequences for therapeutic techniques and results.

Actually we are not yet able to state with assurance that the neurotic process arises from any one of several different roots, or, alternatively, that there is one single trunk which is common to all and from which all of the protean manifestations of the "neuroses" differentiate under the influence of later stressful events and situations. Therefore, we cannot gather together the statistics on the psychotherapy (psychoanalytic or otherwise) even of cases of handwashing compulsion as though all handwashing compulsions were a unit, when one may arise out of an essentially hysterical personality, another out of a psychoneurotic depression, and a third out of a setting which is a way station in the slow evolution of a paranoid schizophrenic psychosis.

If we are to develop techniques which are focused on specific etiologies, we must *determine whether the various psychoneurotic constellations have common or diverse origins,* whether they are opposite sides of a coin minted out of a single metal, whether the therapeutic maneuvers which are focused on initial steps will be identical with or quite different from the therapeutic maneuvers which are needed when we deal with the *tertiary consequences* of earlier events in the evolution of the neurotic process itself. Therapies cannot be compared until we can relate them to uniform psychopathologic sequences. Current theories would indicate that we were trying to evaluate the effects of antibiotics on all illnesses which show fever and rash before we could distinguish between measles and smallpox, or between an initial infection with polio or syphilis and the remote consequences of the destructive scars which they caused. Until all of this basic spadework has been done we cannot even begin to compare the relative efficacy of different techniques.

Nosological Nomenclature

A clarification of our thinking about the essential units of the neurotic processes and their evolution will be further facilitated by discarding once and for all the current misleading phenomenologic nosology of the neuroses. We still accept this unfortunate heritage from the neurology of the nineteenth century; and this in spite of the efforts of Freud, of Adolf Meyer, and of others to modify the existing systematizations. It seems that we must become better naturalists in our study of the neurotic process before we will be ready to become mature students of the dynamics of either etiology or therapy.

Criteria of Change—in Direction, in Intensity, in Rate

The third prerequisite for a mature comparison of the effects of different psychotherapies is to *develop objective indices of change,* i.e., criteria for deciding whether or not there have been basic changes of any kind in the dynamic psychologic processes which underlie patterns of behavior. Changes in behavior can often be induced by so-called "therapeutic" maneuvers without any alteration in the deeper tides which flow from human need and conflict. Such compliant changes in the surface of behavior, however useful and gratifying they may be, are never a sure index of what is going on in the depths. Moreover, criteria of change should not at first be colored by the value judgments which must invest our therapeutic efforts. Our initial concern should be not with whether a change is in the direction of health or of illness but solely with the question of whether or not any change has occurred in the basic psychodynamic equilibria within the personality. Moreover, such criteria will be qualitative before they can be quantified. As long as we lack definitive indicators of change and as long as we lack measuring implements with which to quantify such changes our efforts to compare therapeutic success or failure cannot be conclusive.

The criterion which comes closest to satisfying me personally has not won any wide acceptance even as an abstract concept, and this in spite of the fact that it rests on a hypothesis which is both implicit and obvious in Freud's earlier writings. This working hypothesis is that all human action, feeling, and thought are the result of a continuous, concurrent interplay among conscious, preconscious, and unconscious processes. The dominant role in this concurrent interplay is sometimes held by unconscious processes, sometimes by preconscious and conscious forces, etc., the *dominant position shifting constantly under the influence of many intrinsic and extrinsic forces*. Which combination of these three systems exercises the dominant influence in our general patterns of living and in relation to specific symptomatic structures is the most important fact that we can ascertain about a human being. Consequently, anything which would indicate whether the dominant role is shifting in one direction or another, and the point at which it finally comes to rest, would constitute the most basic criterion of personality change.

I have often pointed out that we need new instruments for estimating the relative roles of these three systems at any moment of existence. Without such tools to give precision to our thinking about psychodynamic relationships we cannot establish even a point of departure from which to measure change. Moreover, such instruments will have additional value for appraising the relative roles of the three sources of psychological processes which interact within the personality on conscious, preconscious, and unconscious levels; to wit, those which have their roots in instinctual needs and their derivatives; those which arise out of identifications within the family group or in society in a broader sense; and those which arise from forces which have been incorporated into superego facets of the personality. These new instruments are needed to give measurable values to our basic concept of psychologic health and illness. All of this has been discussed repeatedly in earlier papers, to which I can only refer here (Kubie, 1947a, 1947b, 1949, 1954).

Estimation of Extrinsic Influences

Finally, I would repeat what I have alluded to many times; namely, that for an accurate comparison of different psychotherapeutic procedures we must be able to estimate also the concurrent influence of forces which arise not within the therapeutic situation but

out of the external situation of a patient's life. In one
illness extrinsic influences may facilitate the therapeutic process. In another and similar illness they may
thwart and undermine therapy. Because these have
been discussed in detail in earlier studies they need
not be reviewed here. But it will be worthwhile to de-
vote thought to the neglected problem of that prepara-
tory planning of the strategy of therapy which is
needed in any effort to control such extrinsic factors.
What I have attempted here is merely to indicate a few
of the essential conditions which must be met in any
precise comparative study of psychotherapeutic successes and failures.

UNSOLVED PROBLEMS

There are so many unsolved problems in
psychoanalytic psychotherapy that it is impossible to
cover them in any single paper. The most that can be
done here is to list with brief comments a few examples of the more pressing problems.

I have already indicated that until we can isolate
and identify with clarity the units both of illness and
of therapy, precise comparison is impossible. I can be
more specific about some of the steps which this will
require.

First, the unitary components of illness must be
sought in directions other than those to which we are
accustomed. I would be concerned with such questions
as early ego identifications and to what extent these
can change in therapy; and also early role diffusions
and how these respond. The phenomena of *multiple*

personalities tend to be overlooked except when they assume melodramatic forms in the relatively rare, fully developed case. Actually, in larval and masked forms this is a universal phenomenon to which almost no attention has been given, either as an ingredient in neuroses and psychoses or with respect to its accessibility to the influence of psychotherapy. Again, in many (and perhaps in everyone) there is a tendency to establish a central emotional position to which the individual returns automatically except when contrary forces push in another direction, yet against which whenever this central position is painful the individual will struggle all his life. The influence of various psychotherapeutic processes on these central affective positions has never been studied. Related to this, in turn, is the phenomenon of *trigger mechanisms*. These are equally universal; yet, with curious naïveté we ordinarily consider only the phobias, although trigger mechanisms can also set off elation, laughter, good humor, anger, depression, obsessional and compulsive furors, explosions of unbridled instinctual demands, sudden delusional states, sleep, and various other dissociative processes. From moment to moment they play an unheralded role in the minutiae of all "normal" living; yet, no one has considered the influence of psychotherapeutic maneuvers of any kind on such trigger mechanisms.

In connection with these trigger mechanisms (of which phobias are the paradigm) there are not only the obvious compulsive, phobic, and obsessional processes but also many *masked processes* of similar nature which ordinarily go unrecognized. Sometimes these exist as a steady stream; sometimes they come in bursts and volleys and then subside. This is another ingredient in the protean manifestations of the neurotic process, to which little attention has been paid nosologically, and none in terms of its responsiveness to the psychotherapies.

In connection with the extraordinary phenomenology of sleep, we have never studied the drift to illness that may occur in the spontaneous dissociated states of falling asleep and of awaking, or for that matter in sleep itself. We have not examined the conditions which determine when sleep will be restorative and integrative, and when it will be a disintegrative process; nor what it is which determines when either influence will carry over into the waking state. How sleep processes alter under psychotherapy has never been studied at all. Directly related to this is the distortion of the symbolic processes which occurs spontaneously in all dissociated states (sleep, hypnosis, under drugs, etc.). Since this *distortion of symbolic relationships* is the essence of the neurosis and of the psychosis, and since it also occurs in the dream, in the neurotic symptoms, and in the psychosis, one might expect that its spontaneous distortion in all of the dissociative processes of normal life would long since have been investigated, if only to provide a solid basis for a fresh study of the impact of psychotherapy on these distortions.

For me these are a few of the hard, subtle, intricate, elusive, and unsolved problems of all psychotherapy, including psychoanalytic psychotherapy. They are of such complexity that when any naïve therapist brings to the total problem of psychotherapy nothing more than some new trick, I confess that I feel only an intense and irritable impatience.

And if we look more closely into the therapeutic process for its ingredients we find that here too the problems which are basic for any comparative evaluation of psychotherapies have for the most part been slighted.

First among these are questions which center around the study of the process of free association as a polling device, i.e., as our only approximation to randomicity in securing relatively unweighted representative samples of psychological processes. Through free associations the roles of deliberate conscious selection and rejection and of automatic preconscious selection and rejection are reduced to a minimum, thus exposing to view the influence of unconscious forces. Yet, there have been no systematic *investigations of the alterations in the stream of free associations* which can be produced by varying interpretations or by varying the total analytic situation or by varying the transference relationships. Nor have we tested the accuracy of our hypotheses concerning such changes by attempting to predict alterations in the stream of free association and by comparing the effect of different techniques on the ratio of accurate to inaccurate predictions.

Even before attempting such studies, however, we must solve *the problems of recording*. These are many and complex. Since it is impossible ever to study all, we must study sample recordings of free associations, only making sure that the samplings are truly representative, relatively random, and statistically adequate. In such samples of recorded free associations we must then study the form, content, continuity, length of run, spacings, clusterings, etc., until we can recognize the basic patterns which would then be the starting point of our predictions. Certainly, without quantitative studies of the ratio of accurate to inaccurate predictions it is quite impossible to estimate the validity of interpretations, or for that matter the relative value of any differing therapeutic procedures.

Another matter of vital importance is a study of the value and the limitation of verbal communications from the patient to the analyst and from the analyst to the patient, i.e., the relative roles of the conscious, preconscious, and unconscious components in all such communications, and the forms which determine which communications carry the affective content of the experience or only the dusty residue which is represented by words. This, in turn, leads to a review of the various forms of memory, from purely verbal memory to the deep reliving of past events as though they were occurring here and now, with an obscuring of those boundaries of time and space which ordinarily separate us from that which is distant. This, in turn, leads directly to a consideration of the many factors which influence the value and limitations of insight.

Such studies will have to be carried on not only in states of full consciousness but also in sleep, under drugs of various kinds, in states of partial hypnoidal dissociation, and under full hypnosis, i.e., in states of induced communicative sleep. All of these are vital in any investigations of the therapeutic process, since everything which can be studied in the state of full conscious awareness and alertness must also be studied in every conceivable state of partial and controlled dissociation.

These are just a few of the basic areas in the psychotherapeutic process which we must explore. They imply also that exhaustive consideration must be given to the strategy of the preparation for therapy, to the organization of the patient's life so as to give therapy an opportunity to function effectively, and to unsolved problems in the interrelating of extramural and intramural practice. These bring up all of the limitations of private practice, some of which I listed above, and the urgency of our need for institutes for basic research in psychoanalytic psychiatry.

REFERENCES

KUBIE, L. S., *et al.* Problems in clinical research: Round table. American *Journal of Orthopsychiatry,* 1947, *17*(2): 196–230.

KUBIE, L. S., BRONNER, A. F., HENDRICK, I., KRIS, E., SHAKOW, D., BROSIN, H. W., BERGMAN, P., and BIBRING, E. The objective evaluation of psychotherapy: Round table. *American Journal of Orthopsychiatry,* 1949, *19* (3), 463–491.

KUBIE, L. S. Modern concept of energy exchange in the central nervous system in relation to the libido theory (read in part before the meeting of the American Psychoanalystic Association, St. Louis, May, 1954).

The Working-through Phase—
Failure to Focus

BERNARD F. RIESS, PH.D.

THE CASE to be described represents a psychotherapeutic failure in the sense that change and improvement were unnecessarily delayed because of the therapist's misperception of the nature of the patient's so-called resistance. With the recognition of a new direction of inquiry and self-understanding, there was immediate change for the better. Although our scientific colleagues may not be happy with the causal inference of this shift, it at least sets up a hypothesis by which future cases can be studied.

I shall try not to specify the precise misperception which triggered the delay so that critics will have some empirical meat on which to sharpen their critical teeth. Perhaps some time there will be an opportunity to compare the inferences from the data presented and to relate these inferences to subsequent changes in the patient.

In introducing this material, it is necessary to state both the orientation which the therapist finds congenial and the stage of the relationship with the patient at which the failure occurred. For me, the most useful and comfortable frame of reference in psychotherapeutic theory is that of so-called classic Freudian psychoanalysis. In the instance to be presented, the patient was seen in an outpatient treatment agency at a frequency of four times a week. The couch was used as a therapeutic locale for the greater part of the treatment process but intermittent face-to-face sessions were introduced when anxiety rose to serious levels.

The crucial phase of treatment (at which time the misperception arose) is the period which has been called the "working-through" stage. It is a frequent, almost invariable, experience of therapists that a time arises during treatment in which no progress is made. The patient knows the pattern of his neurotic behaviors. He is intellectually aware of the symbolic significance of his symptoms; he has accepted the interpretations of his behavior and the analysis of his transference. He has so-called insights, but he cannot translate them into action. This is a frustrating stage to the beginning therapist, who refuses to take comfort from or refuge in the advice of his more experienced colleagues and supervisors that "therapy requires time to jell" or that "the patient must overcome his resistances." To me, it is this period that invalidates the theoretical positions of non-Freudians, because playing all of the stops on the transactional or interpersonal organ does not seem to move the listener to action. The case to be presented briefly now illustrates, I hope, how a theoretical or insufficiently theory-based approach leads to prolonged failure on the patient's part to get into a positive position which is experienced as progress.

The Family Setting

At beginning of treatment, the patient was young, unmarried, 22 years of age, an art student, and earning his living as a letterer in a publishing concern. His father—the patient being an only son—had been an artist of reputation in Europe and barely successful in the United States. Remote from and hypercritical of his son's creative activity, the father was subordinate to his wife, acting variously as her nurse, whipping boy, and domestic worker. John's mother was sickly, querulous, and overprotective of her son, still washing his face and back during his early 20's.

The patient's attitude to his father, at the beginning of treatment, had been one of fear, dependence on him for criticism of every attempt to do anything with visual art, and a pervasive need to please. John felt toward his mother an almost infantile, helpless dependence. He was her child, servant, and willing pawn in her fights with his father.

The reason for John's coming for treatment had been an experience with an army selection board psychiatrist who had called him a homosexual. This label fitted into the patient's self-perception, since he saw himself as small, thin, weak, anemic, and unathletic. His self-ideal at the onset of therapy was the "*Saturday Evening Post* football hero, the all-American youth." In his attempt to reach this goal, he bought elevator shoes and suits with padded shoulders. The allegation of homosexuality panicked him, and, following his basic dependency pattern, he ran for help to the very source of authority that had precipitated the anxiety.

As we saw each other over the following years, John came to realize that his behavior toward authority figures was maladaptive and emanated essentially from his father's unconscious but fairly obvious desire for a girl-child, a substitute for the wife whom he had never really enjoyed. The father therefore effeminized his son, criticized and minimized his achievements, and fought all attempts by John to assert himself. This process of depersonalization was enhanced by the mother's seductiveness and unwillingness to see her son as an independent adult.

Self-Assertion

The extent of the patient's suspiciousness and hostility toward all helping authority figures was manifested in the early months of treatment by his attitude to his therapist. He even called the American Psychological Association in Washington to see whether he could check on my credentials. The presence of the magazine *Nation* in the office was proof to him of my intention to brainwash him and turn him into a traitor. As he developed the courage to talk openly about his hostility, he changed in his overt, nontherapy-hour behavior and even demanded and obtained an increase in both salary and status on the job. In current transactional language, his ego boundaries had expanded through the immersion in a permissive, friendly relationship with a nonpunitive and nonseductive parental substitute. His dreams and fantasies during this period were centered around themes of battle, hostility, and defiance and, as he seemed to progress, they included more explicit and clearly visualized images of his actual parents.

Sexual Problems

With all this seeming improvement, there was one area which appeared to defy change. This was in the sexual field. Any image, situation, or off-color joke which mentioned homosexuality triggered an intense anxiety reaction. Relations with girls were entered into with fear and an expectation of rejection both for not being the ideal American male and for the homosexual picture which he was sure he projected in the minds of girls whom he dated. Repetition of this theme was endless. For months, each session was begun with a query or a dream-recital in which fear of homosexual attack or overture were central. John dug into Kinsey, Ellis, and other so-called authorities on homosexuality to find out whether his body-build, esthetic interests, and family background were similar to self-identified homosexuals. As the therapist I tried to make him see the relationship of the fantasied attacks and fears as distortions of the hostility and guilt centering on his father and mother. The elaborate and repetitive working over of these problems and their patterned projection in behavior had no effect in reducing the anxiety nor in facilitating easy-going heterosexual contacts or even man-woman friendships.

At this time, too, the patient began to wonder whether there was any use in continuing treatment.

Progress had been made, but this block seemed endless and insuperable. Some regression took place in the form of the older questioning of the therapist's competence. More hostility to the therapist also appeared in John's dreams.

My attitude, after six months of this, was also negative. I began to pressure the patient to go out. "At least try to make out with your date," "stop fighting me and, through me, your father," and so on. Vacation was a real gift, since both of us felt that little was being accomplished in the continuation of our relationship.

Upon resuming sessions after the summer, there were weeks of relatively good meetings. The vacation had been pleasant for both of us. My patient had had fairly frequent dates with a wide variety of women, but not one had been really successful or productive of a continuing, not to say meaningful, relationship. Productivity in the vocational area had been good. He had given up his job and was conducting a successful free-lance book-production business which allowed him scope and time for some esthetic as well as financial returns.

However, the honeymoon ended as we had left it in the early summer: more and more hostility, despair, concern with body-image, homosexual panics, gradual withdrawal from social life, and increased questioning about the value of treatment. Four sessions were spent in reviewing all that we thought we knew about John and then began a serious discussion of termination. As was expected, facing the fact of the end of the relationship provided new fears, separation anxieties, and hostile-dependency conflicts. But both of us "knew" that we had reached an impasse.

Let me, at this point, depict briefly the situation as we had reviewed it. Had it not been for a chance observation which occurred at the time of the last session, both John and I would have called the experience at best an incomplete analysis and in a more honest vein an almost complete failure.

Following an anamnestic process, it soon turned out that John saw himself as ineffective in almost all areas, so that the sexual panic was seen as only one phase of the overlying character structure. As one would expect, the dynamism was supplied by an analysis of the development and vicissitudes of the family interactions. Here John learned to see himself as a pawn in a parental battle, and realized that he had used his weak ego to appease his mother and infuriate his father. A classical Oedipal portrait was etched in which the therapist was on occasion seen and/or experienced as a new type of parental figure. This much was clear, and the fear of and hostility to the male was seen as a reaction-formation against jealousy. Generalization of attitudes to males was highlighted by relationships on the job, with friends, and with the therapist.

In the previous discussion, the absence or mention of sexual development and recognition of self as a sexual being may seem pointed. References to this area were fairly frequent. Masturbation constituted the major source of sexual gratification, but even this erotic practice was not often engaged in. Fantasies accompanying autoerotic stimulation consisted of several repeated thematic images. In one set of fantasies, John saw himself as the strong, big, aggressive male pursuing a woman, the latter always plump, buxom, and of Jewish origin. It is significant that in his slangy moments when describing his usually abortive attempts to meet girls, he used the expression "out to get laid" and never "out to lay" or "to screw." So the conflict between the oral dependent, receptive actuality and the fantasied dominant male was observed, discussed, and related by interpretations and insights to the Oedipal structure.

Another theme repeated in masturbating activity was intercourse or sexual play between two masked performers. The mask seemed to be the erotizing factor and little progress was made in unveiling its symbolic significance.

Superego Resistance

It was at this point that the decision seemed to lie in the balance between admission of at least partial failure or a departure into a new line of approach. Since I am compulsively bound to a search of literature when conflict or doubt arises and I was fortuitously busy at that time preparing a series of lectures on the middle phase of therapy, I looked for help in the library. My taking-off point was resistance, and I came upon Freud's article on "Recollection, Repetition and Working Through." Here was a description and classification of resistances some of which seemed to fit the case. I felt we had worked through transference resistance, repression, and resistance to gain by illness, but that we had never really faced the two major sources of blocking that Freud called the *id* and the *superego resistance*. This translated itself for me into a lack of confrontation with the infantile omnipotence-helplessness stage and with the importance of guilt. What my patient was expressing in his sexual fantasies, the masked performers and the motherly lover, was not only a conflict between id and superego but a sort of resolution of the conflict which allowed the maladjustment to continue. In effect, the patient was forcing his mother to be his mistress by compliance and signaling this solution to his conscience by rebelling against it. At the same time, the superego unconsciously used the guilt to keep the primitive drives under control.

All of this sounds highly theory-bound. In practice, I focused upon the patient's repeated pursuit of guilt, his proclivity for situations in which he felt no good while at the same time experiencing erotic satisfaction from his acts. As we worked on this issue, and as he found himself punished not for what he did but for what he prevented himself from doing, he was able to escape from the double bind and to face his Oedipal yearnings without guilt. Now he was able to have intercourse, first with an older woman and then with a peer.

What did I learn from this? My hypothesis about "working through" now is that the difficulties here arise mainly because the therapist allies himself with the superego, avoids facing the real, asocial origin of guilt, and thus reinforces a repetition-compulsion which keeps the patient in treatment because he knows he *should* get better, and the conflict with the source of the "should-antagonist" is intensified.

The Human Factor in Psychoanalysis and Psychotherapy

BENJAMIN B. WOLMAN, PH.D.

WHENEVER I have taught treatment methods to younger colleagues, I have always tried to dissuade them from copying my behavior. Ever so often a less experienced colleague would burst out with a question, "And how would you have treated this case? How would *you* have reacted in this situation?"

Whether it was direct supervision or presentation of cases in a hospital setting, my answer was always the same and almost redundant. "You are not I, and I am not you. Your reacting like me would not have had the same effect on the patient as my reaction has had. Please do not do what I do; do what you can do, keeping in mind your patient and your own resources."

Once a paranoid schizophrenic pulled out a knife at me. He was 6 feet 2 inches tall and weighed 200 pounds. I am slightly over 5 feet 5 inches and weigh 140 pounds. He held a switchblade knife; I had in my hand a Papermate ball-point pen. The odds were on his side, and the outcome of a physical confrontation was easily predictable.

I looked angrily at him and shouted, "Who the hell do you think you are? Put that *thing* on my desk, right away, or I'll never see you again!" He looked at me meekly and put "the thing" on my desk. He probably lost his nerve and thought at this moment, "Who the hell am I?" Possibly he was afraid that I would reject him and refuse to see him again, and, being very much attached to me, he cried and apologized. Another therapist, who didn't have this kind of close relationship with the patient and enough self-confidence, and whose voice would tremble and his eyes show fear, would probably have failed in this dramatic encounter.

The outcome of any given situation depends on the nature of the participants and the character of their interaction. Each psychotherapeutic and psychoanalytic process is, in a way, an unrepeatable event, an idiophenomenon, and its predictability depends on a field-theoretical grasping of the totality of the interactional factors. Prognosis depends not only on the patient but also on who is his therapist.

One cannot, therefore, learn by imitation even when the case descriptions are detailed and illuminating. Once I had an argument with a young psychoanalyst whom I was supervising. He frequently quoted Freud's papers on technique despite my insistence on the *nonrepeatability* of clinical experiences. Once, describing his new patient, he exclaimed enthusiastically: "This is *exactly* the case as described by Herr Professor Doctor Sigmund Freud in *Gesammelte Schriften!*" (The German was obviously for my benefit.)

I could not agree with him, for neither Freud nor his patient could ever have been exactly duplicated. I suggested to my young friend that he pay less attention to Freud's patients and concentrate on his own intellectual frame of reference, his own personality, and on the *real* personalities of his patients.

Of course, one may get useful hints from case descriptions. I believe, however, that one may learn more from the description of a therapist's difficulties or problem areas than from self-praise. Thus, let me describe some of the cases where I faced serious difficulties with my patients. All of us make mistakes, but unless we become aware of them we may never be able to correct them.

THE NATURE OF TRANSFERENCE

I shall divide my remarks into three parts: (1) failures arising from the patients; (2) failures resulting from shortcomings related to my own personality traits; and (3) failures related to sociological factors.

The rationale of my work is based on a certain modification of the psychoanalytic method. I call my method "interactional" (Wolman, 1967a), to stress my belief that the psychoanalytic process is a process of interaction. The psychoanalyst wittingly or unwittingly participates in this interaction. He always manipulates the transference and, as much as he can, also his own countertransference.

Transference is an emotional attitude to objects and people in which one relives his past experiences. People often repeat past experiences and act as if the present situation were a replica of the past. Men often fall in love with girls to whom they ascribe physical and mental traits which they ascribed in childhood to their mothers. Some men transfer Oedipal hate into a hate of superiors in the army or in an office. Preference for colors, melodies, fashions, odors, people, and places is often a product of transference.

A great many likes and dislikes originate in transference, but they inevitably affect the *here-and-now* behavior. The here-and-now behavior includes transference and nontransference elements. Human interaction is a multiple-level process; some elements of human attitudes are rational, dictated by the present needs and circumstances, and some are transference phenomena based on irrational residues of the past. Transference is but a fraction of the totality of interaction; when a patient expects instinctual gratification in a psychoanalytic situation, it is mainly because he has transferred infantile instinctual demands to the analyst. But the adult patient is not an infant, and his instinctual demands are here-and-now demands that form an integral part of his total interaction with the psychoanalyst.

Instead of participating unwittingly in this interaction the psychoanalyst should become aware of the fact that his words and his silences, his activity or passivity, are an inevitable part of the psychoanalytic process. F. Alexander and T. French (1946) suggested that transference be regulated; I believe that *it is always regulated by the analyst,* but he is not always aware of this.

Every psychoanalytic treatment, as Fenichel put it, is "based on the analyst's influence on the patient" (1945, page 447). I suggest that this influence be made explicit, and that the analyst become aware of the nature of his influence. Psychoanalysts regulate transference by imposing the "basic rule," by suggesting the reclining position, by saying or not saying "How are you?" and even by smiling or not smiling during the session.

Several years ago I sat in a locked ward in a mental hospital and observed interindividual processes. Although my policy was one of a strict nonparticipant observation, my very presence on the ward influenced the behavior of the patients. In the one-to-one relationship everything pertaining to the analyst must affect the patient and influence the transference, irrespective of the analyst's intentions.

Marmor criticized the classic approach. He wrote, "The original theoretical dictum that the analyst must be a shadowy, neutral, impersonal, and a value-free figure is coming to be recognized not only as a practical impossibility but even as being in some instances at least of questionable therapeutic value" (Marmor, 1960). My contention is that no analyst is really "shadowy, or neutral," but he must become aware of who he is and what he is doing. I suggest, instead of the intuitive approach, a carefully chosen therapeutic strategy related to the clinical types and levels of deterioration.

Freud's difficulty with schizophrenics as compared with Federn's success with them is a case in point. The insistence on a reclining position facilitated topographic regression; this regression was promoted even more by the "basic rule" of free association; and finally, the analyst's remoteness and silence contributed to the schizophrenic tension and withdrawal. No wonder Freud believed that schizophrenia is a nontransference disorder (Freud, 1915–1917; Fenichel, 1945, Chapter 18). But Federn, who admitted schizophrenics to his home, witnessed most profound transference (1952). In my own work with schizophrenics, described in a monograph (Wolman, 1967b), I have advocated the rule of *getting involved with the patient's cause without getting involved with the patient in any personal way* (avoidance of countertransference). Transference, as repetition of past cathexes, greatly depends on the past interindividual experiences. In transference, the patient reenacts the pathogenesis of neurosis. Freud was aware of the difference in the types of transference. I have been trying to make this awareness more explicit.

Patient's Difficulties

HOMOSEXUALITY   I view homosexuality not as a clinical entity but as a syndrome associated with a variety of mental disorders. The way people experience their sexual life reflects their total personality structure, their estimate of themselves, and their attitude toward others. Sexuality, except for masturbation, is an interindividual process that includes a variety of overt behavioral patterns and a multitude of covert phenomena, and can be found at any age, social group, and culture. *"Perverted sexuality,"* wrote Freud, "is nothing else but infantile sexuality magnified and separated into its component parts" (Freud, 1915–1917, page 272).

Sex is a most intimate human relationship and must

not be reduced to its physiological foundations. One becomes homosexual because he or she was unable to outgrow the "polymorphous perversion" of infancy and failed to mature and attain proper psychosexual identification.

Homosexuality is a cluster of symptoms rather than a clinical entity; one can find homosexuality among schizophrenics, manic-depressives, psychopaths, and in practically any other clinical type.

Some time ago (Wolman, 1966) I suggested dividing all nonorganic mental disorders into three types. In the *psychopathic* or *hyperinstrumental* type, libido is self-hypercathected and destrudo is object directed. In the *hypervectorial* (the *obsessive, schizoid,* and *schizophrenic*) type, libido is object-hypercathected and destrudo is directed inwardly. The third type, the *dysmutual,* includes *hysterics, cycloids,* and *depressives* who swing from love to hate in self and object cathexes (Wolman, 1967a). (See the accompanying Table.)

The psychopaths (hyperinstrumentals) are "polymorphous perverts." They follow the "pleasure principle" and practice indiscriminate sexuality. They have few inhibitions: they masturbate, seduce minors, practice incest, and indulge in any available perversions. Some of them call themselves "bisexual," but they don't shy away from any sexual practice, including rape and sadism as long as they can get away with it (Wolman, 1966c).

The manic-depressives (dysmutuals) are usually the rejected children who identify with the rejecting parent of the same sex. Quite often their homosexual tendencies are associated with sado-masochistic desires to suffer and to punish those whom they love (Wolman, 1966a).

In the obsessive and schizophrenic type (hypervectorials) homosexuality is usually a result of the confusion in psychosocial roles. The parents of schizophrenics are demanding and seductive, and involve the child in their emotional problems, expecting the child to

CLASSIFICATION OF SOCIOGENIC MENTAL DISORDERS

Types \ Levels	Hyperinstru-mentalism I	Dysmutual M	Hypervectorialism V
Neurotic level	HYPERINSTRU-MENTAL NEUROSIS (narcissistic and depressive neuroses)	DYSMUTUAL NEUROSIS (dissociative and conversion neuroses)	HYPERVECTORIAL NEUROSIS (obsessional, phobic, and neurasthenic neuroses)
Character neurotic level	HYPERINSTRU-MENTAL CHARACTER NEUROSIS (sociopathic or psychopathic character)	DYSMUTUAL CHARACTER NEUROSIS (cyclothymic and hysteric character)	HYPERVECTORIAL CHARACTER NEUROSIS (schizoid and compulsive character)
Latent psychotic level	LATENT HYPER-INSTRUMENTAL PSYCHOSIS (psychopathic reactions bordering on psychosis)	LATENT DYSMUTUAL PSYCHOSIS (borderline manic-depressive psychosis)	LATENT VECTORIASIS PRAECOX (borderline and latent schizophrenia)
Manifest psychotic level	HYPERINSTRU-MENTAL PSYCHOSIS (psychotic psychopathy, and moral insanity)	DYSMUTUAL PSYCHOSIS (manifest manic-depressive psychosis)	VECTORIASIS PRAECOX (manifest schizophrenia)
Dementive level	Collapse of Personality Structure		

compensate them for their marital frustrations. When the incestuous parent is of the same sex, homosexual identification may develop. In some cases *paranoid projection* develops as a reaction to a panic stemming from a heterosexual or homosexual incestuous situation. Whenever both parents act seductively, their schizophrenic offspring may be confused in regard to his own sex and develop both hetero– and homosexual desires.

TREATMENT OF HOMOSEXUALS The therapist must treat not the homosexual behavior but the patient as a total person. The technique must be modified according to the clinical type. Thus, for instance, in the treatment of schizophrenic homosexuals the emphasis is on schizophrenia and not on homosexuality. Schizophrenics are overinvolved with one or both parents and, thus, unable to establish their own identity. In deep transference the schizophrenic expects love, forgiveness, and care from the therapist; some schizophrenic patients wish to be fed and taken care of by the therapist. They often develop infantile, symbiotic attachments. Many schizophrenic patients express powerful hetero- or homosexual desires, reflecting the incestuous involvement with parents and the wish to enact these desires in the therapeutic sessions.

I believe that such a powerful transference must be treated by a truthful and simple explanation of the nature of the therapist-patient relationship. When I turned down the love advances of a female patient, I pointed to my professional duties. The patient took the explanation calmly; she understood that I did not reject her as a female or as a person. She comprehended the *reality* of the therapeutic relationship and came to terms with reality. She felt frustrated, but she understood that my attitude was *right* (superego) and *realistic* (ego).

The resolution of the negative Oedipal entanglements must often be postponed until the patient's ego has gained adequate control. Ego-supportive therapy and fostering of self-esteem are the choice methods. The strength of the patient's ego is the chief determinant as to how far one should go in interpretation of unconscious material.

Handling of the fear of rejection is the focal issue in the treatment of manic-depressives (dysmutuals). These patients swing from positive to negative transference: as long as they imagine that the analyst loves them they are in a blissful euphoria, but even this mostly imaginary "love" does not last long. The manic-depressives are love addicts, and they demand attention, love, and tangible proof of the analyst's alleged love for them. A male hysteric who developed a homosexual crush in transference demanded an increased number of sessions and the right to call me several times a day; he even planned to take an apartment nearby. A young woman complained: "You are nice to all your patients, but I am not just a patient. I love you. Why can't you make me happy?"

Woe to the analyst who lets himself be drawn into the treadmill of the emotional ups and downs of a manic-depressive patient! The detached, objective, matter-of-fact treatment of transference combined with judicious interpretation of resistance and transference is the best method. A gradual acceptance of the detached relationship of the analyst combined with the insight into the patient's homosexual identification with the rejecting parent of the opposite sex may help the patient to outgrow his infantile sexuality.

In the treatment of psychopaths (hyperinstrumentals), fostering of the superego may seem necessary. Normality implies social adjustment and a reasonable balance of inter- and intra-individual cathexes. Normality includes a balanced love for oneself and others and a balance of criticism of oneself and others; and a rational superego is an indispensable part of a healthy personality.

The analyst faces a complex task in treatment of psychopathic homosexuals. His silent permissiveness may be misinterpreted as siding with their id, but overt expressions of disapproval by the analyst may lead to the inclusion of the analyst in the paranoid picture of a world conspiracy against the patient, who believes in his innocence. The analyst must take a stand and help in developing the patient's superego, but he must wait until the transference is sufficiently strong. Interpretation must wait until the patient is ready to accept it, and even then firmness must be combined with caution. An excessively passive or a too early and too active intervention may lead to a breaking off of the treatment.

FEMALE HOMOSEXUALITY Male homosexuals, as a rule, develop positive and negative transference which could be interpreted and worked through. When a manic-depressive homosexual criticized me for being short, middle-aged, and Jewish and emphatically repeated how much he disliked me, it was pretty obvious that he was sexually attracted to me and his derogatory remarks were simply reaction formation; soon he began telling me how much he loved me and how much he desired me physically.

I have had, however, definite difficulties with female homosexuals of all three types. A hypervectorial, latent schizophrenic female patient competed with me in group therapy, trying to take over my role. She tried to gain control over other people, but, according to her, she was getting along well with me. She endeavored to ward off her sexual impulses by being exceedingly hostile to other females. She had a long history of fights with her mother, whom she adored, desired, and fought. She viewed her father as an insignificant figure, controlled by her mother, and tried to repeat her mother's domineering attitude in the psychotherapeutic relationship. She never developed sufficient attachment to me, and when I prematurely tried to interpret her peculiar attitude to me, she broke off.

Once I had in analysis a 29-year-old, good-looking, and highly sophisticated lesbian patient. She was a versatile and aggressive newspaper editor. Her transference was rather peculiar, for most of the time she liked me, but was suspicious and jealous of my female patients. As all latent manic-depressives (the cyclic or dysmutual type), she had strong paranoid tendencies. On a few occasions she concocted dramatic stories in which I was allegedly unfaithful to her. She was seductive and aggressive at the same time. She accused me of having affairs with all my female patients, and especially one young and very attractive girl. Soon, through dreams and free associations it became clear that the lesbian editor had used me as a cover for her passionate love for the young girl. The lesbian patient began to compete with me for the alleged love of the other girl. She accused me of rejecting her and having a love affair with the younger girl, and, before I learned how to cope with the problem, she broke off.

I had considerable difficulties with a psychopathic, hyperinstrumental female homosexual. She was 26, charming, witty, but overconcerned with her looks and a hypochondriac, as many psychopaths are. She related to me in a very friendly, easygoing fashion. She confided in me, showing practically no inhibition or resistance. She was polite and friendly, but seemed not to care too much what I might have thought of her. She treated me as a friend whom she could trust and tell her little sexual secrets. Obviously, she was as at ease in my office as in her own home. Sometimes she seemed to overlook my presence, ignoring the nature of our relationship. I was just another man, and men meant nothing to her. She walked like a male and talked like a male, and I was supposed to be her buddy.

In a complete lack of any involvement on her part, our therapeutic relationship broke down pretty soon. She found nothing exciting with respect to me; apparently she gave up because she was involved with girls and was unable to develop adequate transference to me.

The inability to develop adequate transference to a person of the opposite sex seems to me to be the crux of the matter. Thus, my impression is that homosexual females are better off with female analysts than with male analysts. In *"Homosexuality in a Woman"* (1920) Freud pointed out the peculiar type of transference in homosexual women that aims at pleasing and betraying the father figure. They may show a great deal of intellectual understanding without any real change in emotions, attitude, and behavior. Homosexual female patients seem to be determined to defy the male analyst and, thus, to defeat him.

Freud wrote:

In reality she transferred to me the deep antipathy to men she had suffered from her father. Bitterness against men is as a rule easy to gratify upon the analyst; it need not evoke any violent emotional manifestations, it simply expresses itself in rendering futile all his endeavors and in clinging to the neurosis. I know from experience how difficult it is to make the patient understand just this mute kind of symptomatic behavior and to make him aware of this latent, and often exceedingly strong, hostility without endangering the treatment. So as soon as I recognized the girl's attitude to her father, I broke off the treatment and gave the advice that, if it was thought worth while to continue the therapeutic efforts, it should be done by a woman (Freud, 1920).

My Own Difficulties

EARLY SUCCESS The second type of difficulty I encounter is related not to patients but to myself, to my limited ability to perceive nonverbal communication, which seems to be one major prerequisite for success in treating mental patients. I believe that I have been quite successful with schizophrenic patients and have been more or less capable of sensing what was on their mind even when their speech was incoherent or when they were mute. I have described my technique in a monograph (Wolman, 1967b), and yet I can not say I am always successful. In all my years of practice I did not have any suicides and in the last 10 years I had no relapses in schizophrenics whom I discharged after prolonged treatment, but I have had astounding difficulties with some patients.

Several years ago I had a paranoid schizophrenic in treatment. Although he was occasionally violent at home he related to me in a most friendly manner. I hoped to help him, and I believed that we had developed good rapport and that we were making good progress. I hoped to pull him out of his social isolation, his autistic mannerisms and paranoic ideas about himself and the world around him.

As we continued working, he became more and more demanding. I believe in the necessity of transference under control, especially with schizophrenics. Somehow I was not cautious enough, and allowed his transference to become too intense. The patient became too attached to me; he even stopped beating his family, not because his ego was capable of controlling aggressive impulses but because he knew that I would not like it. I became his superego, too early and too much.

He somehow got my private home telephone number. He called me several times, day and night. Once he woke me at three o clock in the morning just to tell me that he was very happy that I was his doctor. I must confess that I did not share his happy feelings, and for a while I tried to reason with him. Soon he was calling every hour, day and night. He was angry that I did not interrupt my sessions with other patients and refused to speak with him. He became abusive to my secretary. Finally, I got impatient; I had obviously overestimated the initial success and strength of transference.

PATIENCE I once made a great deal of progress with a girl patient. She was a severe, simple deterioration case of schizophrenia. We had developed good rapport and she began to take an interest in life and to participate in many things from which she had completely withdrawn. She even took a job. The only thing that was causing difficulty was her coming for appointments too early, usually an hour or two or even three ahead of our schedule and expecting me to see her right away. Somehow she complied with the rule that, if she came when another patient was in my office, she had to sit around for a couple of hours and wait. However, she disturbed my secretary and annoyed everybody else, but gradually we were coming to terms.

Again, the question was of her overdemandingness and my inability to cope with her. Once I told her that I had to go on a vacation. She looked at me and said, "You do not look so terribly pale. You look well, and you do not need a vacation."

I said, "But do you mind my going for a vacation?"

She said, "I certainly do. I need you, and you *better* stay here."

The day before I left for vacation, at the last session, she told me, "You are going to hide from me. You know I love you very much and you are going to run away."

That night she came to my office and waited for me all night long. The doorman told her that I was not there. When I came back after a week she called me and said, "If I cannot find you whenever I want, you are not my doctor, and that is all."

I believe that all schizophrenics are basically curable. My inability to cope with the difficulties was not related to lack of skill or knowledge, but because of my not being patient enough with patients.

Schizophrenics become incurable when they cannot find someone sufficiently skillful, tactful, considerate, and patient to be able to deal with their unbelievably complex, difficult, and exasperatingly demanding behavior.

THE VOICE OF UNCONSCIOUS   The patient, Dr. J., was a biologist with a Doctor of Science degree. His knowledge of biochemistry, pharmacology, and physiology was astounding. Originally he planned to become a physician, but he was more interested in research than in practice. He spoke with authority on issues of his competence, and psychosomatic medicine was one of his favorite topics. He was a borderline manic-depressive (paramutual latent psychotic) with a strong self-destructive tendency. His professional career was inconsistent and spotty; after long periods of hard work, he would abandon his projects, run way, and turn to something else. Apparently, he avoided people and shied away from success and then rationalized his defeats.

Once he began complaining about nausea and loss of appetite; he proudly declared that he had developed *anorexia nervosa* and was pleased with his new symptoms.

I disagreed with his self-diagnostic statements. I believe that physical diseases can strike everyone, and neurotics are not immune to TB, pneumonia, and typhoid fever. I have always been opposed to the throwing of all physical symptoms into the wastebasket of psychosomatics. In all the years of my practice, whenever a patient complained of pain or ailment, I always demanded a thorough medical examination. Accordingly I asked Dr. J. to consult his physician. He chided me. "I knew," he said sarcastically, "that you would send me for a physical. That's your old-fashioned philosophy; body comes first."

However, upon my insistence he went to see his family physician. Next day he reported triumphantly: "My doctor could not find anything wrong with me. It's all in my mind. It's psychosomatic, positive."

As time went on, his complaints became more frequent, and he began to lose weight. I worried about him, for his symptoms did not look psychosomatic to me. I sent him for a physical checkup, this time to an internist with whom I closely cooperated. The report was optimistic, diagnosing a mild gastrointestinal trouble, and a medicine was prescribed. Although I kept on insisting on a *thorough* checkup, I tried to convince myself that my worries were irrational. The patient, however, adamantly refused to go for further examinations, and I was torn by an inner conflict; my conscious sided with the internist but my unconscious was full of worries.

A week passed, and Dr. J. reported a strange dream. In his dream his brother, with whom he had strongly identified, was hit in the kidneys by a bomb and was dying. At this point I became absolutely convinced that Dr. J. had cancer of the kidneys or some other serious kidney disease.

I decided to act immediately. I did not communicate my suspicions to Dr. J., but I put to him an ultimatum: either he immediately go for a GI series or I would refuse to see him any longer. I sent him to a top internist. The examination discovered cancer of the kidneys. He was hospitalized immediately and, unfortunately, never came back.

It was a terrible shock. One gets attached to a patient, and I felt horribly about Dr. J. I should have been more inclined to listen to the voice of my unconscious. Were I more determined, less influenced by the two physicians, I would have said, "Go to a top specialist, or I will refuse ever to see you again." I did say that the last time he came to my office, immediately after he told me the dream. I doubt whether an early intervention on my part could have helped, but even today I feel sad when I think of poor Dr. J.

Sociological Factors

There is still another category of patients whom I failed. These are patients whom I never saw. When I was a young man, I had the ambition to become a doctor for poor people. As a young psychotherapist I worked with poor people because they could not afford a more expensive therapist. I can't claim too much success in my early years of practice; it takes years before one acquires proper skills and learns by experience.

Today I believe I know more, but poor people cannot come to see me any longer. In the long years of research and practice I have acquired skill and experience, and only wealthy people can afford my services. I can't help wondering whether all that I do has much meaning, because my skills are available only for the wealthy. There is no doubt that wealthy people are as often in mental trouble as poor ones, and they need help, but why discriminate against the poor?

Sometimes I wonder whether the one-to-one relationship of psychoanalysis and psychotherapy isn't too exclusive for our times when millions need help and seek it. The time has come when we have to think about completely different methods, geared to the *society as a whole*. Our work may be a luxury of bygone days: to sit in one's office charging high fees and seeing one wealthy patient at a time may be tantamount to missing something very urgent. Perhaps group therapy, family therapy, community therapy, and above all, prevention of mental disorders represent the contemporary *Zeitgeist*. We are not in "practice"; we are in *service*. I failed most those patients whom I never had the chance to see at all.

REFERENCES

ALEXANDER, F., and T. FRENCH, *Psychoanalytic Therapy*. New York: Ronald Press, 1946.

FEDERN, P. *Ego Psychology and the Psychoses*. New York: Basic Books, 1952.

FENICHEL, O. *The Psychoanalytic Theory of Neurosis*. New York: Norton, 1945.

FREUD, S. Homosexuality in a Woman (1920), *Collected Papers*. London: Hogarth Press, 1924.

FREUD, S. *Introductory Lectures on Psycho-Analysis* (1915–1917). New York: Perma Giants, 1935.

MARMOR, J. The reintegration of psychoanalysis into psychiatric practice. *Archives of General Psychiatry*, 1960, 3:569–574.

WOLMAN, B. B. Dr. Jekyll and Mr. Hyde: A new theory of the manic-depressive disorder. *Transactions of the New York Academy of Science*, 1966, **28:** 1020–1032 (a).

WOLMAN, B. B. Transference and countertransference as interindividual cathexis. *Psychoanalytic Review*, 1966, **53:**255–256 (b).

WOLMAN, B. B. Classification of mental disorders. *Acta Psychotherapeutica*, 1966, 14:50–65 (c).

WOLMAN, B. B. Interactional psychoanalysis. In B. B. Wolman (ed.), *Psychoanalytic Techniques: A Handbook for the Practicing Psychoanalyst*. New York: Basic Books, 1967 (a).

WOLMAN, B. B. *Vectoriasis Praecox or the Group of Schizophrenias*. Springfield, Ill.: Charles C. Thomas, 1967 (b).

CONTRIBUTORS

ARNOLD BERNSTEIN, Ph.D.

Professor of Psychology, Queens College of the City University of New York

Consultant in the Department of Psychiatry, Metropolitan Hospital Center, New York Medical College

Co-Author, *Anatomy of Psychotherapy* (1960)
Patterns in Human Interaction (1969)
Mystification and Drug Misuse (1971)

HENRY BRILL, M.D.

Director, Pilgrim State Hospital

Co-Author, "Neuropsychopharmacology", (with P. Deniker, H. Hippins, and P. B. Bradley), *Excerpta Medica Foundation* (1967)
Drugs and Youth (1969) (with J. Paul Smith and C. A. Thomas) "The Impact of Modern Chemotherapy on Hospital Organization, Psychiatric Care, and Public Health Policies" (with R. E. Patton) *Proceedings of the Third World Conference of Psychiatry* (1964)

EDWARD GLOVER, M.D., LL. D., F.B.P.S.

Honorary Member, American Psychoanalytic Association

Honorary Consulting Physician, Portman Clinic, London

Co-founder and Chairman, Institute for the Study and Treatment of Delinquency, London

Co-founder and Co-editor, *British Journal of Criminology,* London

Author, *The Technique of Psychoanalysis* (1955)
On the Early Development of Mind (1956)

EDWARD J. HORNICK, M.D.

Associate Professor of Psychiatry, Albert Einstein College of Medicine

Author, "How Teenagers, Their Parents and Their Doctors Can All Grow Up", *Marriage Counseling in Medical Practice* (1964)

"Lunar Effects on Mental Illness: The Relationship of Moon Phases to Psychiatric Emergencies", *American Journal of Psychiatry* (1968)

LAWRENCE S. KUBIE, M.D., D.Sc.

Clinical Professor of Psychiatry, University of Maryland School of Medicine

Senior Associate in Research and Training, The Sheppard and Enoch Pratt Hospital

Author, *Practical and Theoretical Aspects of Psychoanalysis* (1950)

"Problems and Techniques of Psychoanalytic Validation and Progress," *Psychoanalysis as Science* (1952)

Neurotic Distortion of The Creative Process (Porter Lectures) (1958)

The Riggs Story (1960)

STANLEY LESSE, M.D., Med. Sc.D.

Editor-in-Chief, *American Journal of Psychotherapy*

President, Association for the Advancement of Psychotherapy

Author, *Anxiety: Its Components, Development and Treatment* (1970)

An Evaluation of the Results of the Psychotherapies (1968)

BERNARD F. RIESS, Ph.D.

Director of Research, Postgraduate Center for Mental Health,

Author, *New Directions in Mental Health* (1969)

Co-editor, *Progress in Clinical Psychology* (with L. A. Abt)

Editor, *International Newsletter in Mental Health Research*

LEON J. SAUL, M.D.

Emeritus Professor of Psychiatry, Medical School of the University of Pennsylvania

Emeritus Training and Supervising Analyst, Philadelphia
Institute of Psychoanalysis
Psychiatric Consultant, Swarthmore College
Honorary Consultant, Institute of the Pennsylvania Hospital
Author, *Emotional Maturity* (1971)
The Hostile Mind (1956)
Fidelity and Infidelity (1967)

AARON STEIN, M.D.

Clinical Professor of Psychiatry, The Mount Sinai School of
Medicine of the City University of New York
Attending Psychiatrist, The Mount Sinai Hospital
Author, "The Nature and Significance of Interaction in
Group Psychotherapy", *International Journal of Group
Psychotherapy* (1970)
"Group Interaction and Group Psychotherapy in
a General Hospital", *The Mount Sinai Journal of Medicine* (1971)

HANS H. STRUPP, Ph.D.

Professor of Psychology, Vanderbilt University
Author, *Psychotherapists in Action* (1960)
Patients View Their Psychotherapy (1969) (with
R. Fox and K. Lessler)

EARL G. WITENBERG, M.D.

Director, Fellow, Training and Supervising Analyst, The
William Alanson White Institute of Psychiatry, Psycho-
analysis and Psychology
Editor, *An Outline of Psychoanalysis* (1955) (with C. Thomp-
son and M. Mazer)
Editor, *The William Alanson White Institute Twenty-Fifth
Anniversary Volume* (1971)
Author, "The Interpersonal Approach to Treatment with
Particular Emphasis on the Obsessional," *Psychoanalytic
Techniques* (1967)
"The Interpersonal and Cultural Approaches,"
American Handbook of Psychiatry (1959)

BENJAMIN B. WOLMAN, Ph.D.

Professor of Psychology, Long Island University Doctoral Program in Clinical Psychology

Editor, *International Journal of Group Tensions*

Editor, *Psychoanalytic Techniques: A Handbook for the Practicing Psychoanalyst*

Author, *Contemporary Theories and Systems in Psychology* (1960)

Vectoriasis Praecox or the Group of Schizophrenias (1966)

The Unconscious Mind: The Meaning of Freudian Psychology (1968)

Children without Childhood (1970)

Index of Names

Adler, A., 9, 21–34, 54, 57, 167
Adler, K. A., 22
Alexander, F., 95, 102, 235, 252
Andrews, J. D. W., 88, 102

Bernstein, A., 160–176, 253
Bleuler, E., 21
Breuer, J., 166
Brill, H., 153–159, 253
Brücke, E. W. von, 166

Clews, H., 61, 69
Colby, K. M., 76, 102

Ellis, H., 226
Erikson, E., 93
Evans, M., 52
Eysenck, H. J., 72, 75, 102

Federn, P., 236, 237, 252
Fenichel, O., 235, 237, 252
Ferenczi, S., 94, 166
Fliess, W., 27, 166, 167
Fox, R. E., 91, 103
Frank, J. D., 44, 51, 52
French, T. M., 95, 102, 235, 252
Freud, A., 43, 52
Freud, S., viii, 3–20, 23, 30, 38, 43,
    48, 50, 52–54, 57, 74, 77, 93, 94,
    100, 109–111, 116–120, 125–128,
    133, 134, 143, 152, 161–169, 171,
    172, 176, 202, 213, 229, 230, 233,
    234, 236, 237, 245, 252
Fromm, E., 94
Fromm–Reichmann, F., 93, 102, 202

Gill, M. M., 40, 42, 52
Gliedman, L. H., 52
Glover, E., 50, 52, 131–152, 253
Goertzel, V., 52
Greenson, R. R., 40, 52

Hamilton, D. M., 44
Heine, R. W., 30
Helmholtz, H. L. F. von, 166, 167
Hoch, P. H., 44
Horney, K., 53, 94
Hornick, E. J., 193–201, 253

Jones, E., 167, 168, 176
Jung, C. G., 57, 166, 167

Kinsey, A. C., 226
Klein, M., 94
Knight, K. P., 75, 103
Knight, R. P., 44, 52
Koren, L., 44, 52
Kubie, L. S., 177, 192, 202–221, 254

Lesse, S., 53–70, 254
Lessler, K., 91, 103
Lewin, K., viii

Marmor, J., 236, 252
Martin, P. W., 168, 176
Marx, K., 63
Matarazzo, J. D., 76, 103
Meyer, A., 213
Meynert, T., 166
Moreno, J. L., 202

Nunberg, H., 44, 52

Oberndorf, C. P., 44

Paul, G. L., 81–86, 90, 91, 103
Pestalozzi, J. F., 34
Procrustes, 195

Rado, S., 94
Rangell, L., 40, 52
Rank, O., 94
Reich, A., 44, 52
Riess, B. F., 222–231, 254
Riviere, J., 3

Saul, L. J., 107–130, 254
Schick, A., 55, 57, 70
Schiller, F., 25
Searles, H., 194–195
Sharpe, E., 94
Silverberg, W. V., 94
Simonides, 25
Stein, A., 37–52, 255
Stekel, W., 57
Stendhal, 30
Stone, L., 42, 52
Spitz, R. A., 94
Strupp, H. H., 71–103, 255
Sullivan, H. S., 53, 94
Szasz, T. S., 76, 101, 103

Tarachow, S., 37, 40, 42, 43, 48, 50–
    52
Tolstoy, L., 6

Wallach, M. S., 91, 103
Wallerstein, R. S., 44, 48, 52
Weigert, E., 168, 171, 176
Weininger, O., 30
Whyte, W. H., 70
Witenberg, E. G., 177–192, 255
Wogan, M., 91, 103
Wolf, W., 54, 70
Wolman, B. B., 52, 77, 103, 232–252,
    256
Wolpe, J., 82, 103

Index of Subjects

Abulia, 27
Acting out, 109, 112, 194, 200
Adaptation (adaptive), 25, 57, 61, 108
Adolescence, 200
Aggression (aggressive), 22, 229, 243, 246
Amnesia, 156, 157
Analytic therapists, 75, 92
Anorexia nervosa, 249
Anxiety, 40, 46, 47, 79, 81–85, 88, 89, 92, 94, 96, 116, 119, 122, 159, 178–180, 187–191, 196, 210, 223, 225, 226
Anxiety phobias, 142
Authority (figure), 89, 128, 158, 225
Autism (autistic), 21, 246

Behavior modification, 72, 73, 86, 101
Behavior therapist (behaviorist), 75, 79, 86, 88
Behavior therapy, 76, 81

Castration complex (castration anxiety), 116, 169, 200
Catatonic, 154–156
Catharsis, 203
Cathexes (libidinal), 39
Claustrophobia, 210
Client-centered therapy, 71, 86
Communism, 67
Compassion, 160–176
Compulsive (compulsion), 16, 116, 170, 211, 212, 217, 239
Conditioning, 112
Conscious (consciousness), 10, 19, 30, 124, 168, 182, 202, 203, 214, 215, 219, 220, 250
Conversion, 116, 239
Countertransference, viii, ix, 5, 11, 43, 45–51, 115, 120, 121, 127, 128, 134, 160–165, 169, 171, 174, 192, 194, 199, 201, 203, 207, 234, 237
Cycloid (cyclic), 238, 243
Cyclothymic, 27, 239

Deconditioning, 113
Defenses, 38, 109, 143, 146, 147, 186
Delusion (delusional), 126, 217
Dementive, 239
Dependent (dependency), 61, 64, 88, 115, 123, 171, 173, 186–188, 208, 224, 228, 229

Depression (depressive), 46, 92, 111, 119, 122, 142, 147, 155, 184, 188, 196, 210, 217, 238, 239
Depressive symptoms, 48, 49
Destrudo, 238
Dissociation (dissociative), 185, 217, 218, 220, 239
Dynamic (dynamically), 24, 31, 44, 51, 53, 58, 61, 73, 86, 90, 111, 115, 119, 122, 126, 127, 156, 193, 211, 213, 228
Dynamic therapist, 86–88
Dysmutual, 238, 239, 241, 243, 248

Ego, 45, 51, 61, 64, 111, 113, 117, 118, 126, 143, 166, 168, 202, 216, 225, 228, 241, 246
Ego identity, 114
Ego strength, 38, 39, 65, 200
Ejaculatio praecox, 32
Existentialistic approaches to psychotherapy, 76–77

Field theory, viii, 233
Fixations, 17, 114
Free associations, 58, 156, 157, 219, 236, 244
Fugue state, 175

Group ego, 59, 64, 65
Group sociodynamics, 55, 69

Hebephrenic, 31
Heterosexual, 226, 240
Homosexual, 198, 224, 226, 227, 237–245
Hostility, 21, 42, 109, 110, 112, 116, 121, 122, 159, 170, 187, 225–228, 243, 245
Humanistic approaches to psychotherapy, 76–77
Hyperinstrumental, 238, 239, 242, 244
Hypervectorial, 238, 239, 243
Hypochondriasis (hypochondriac), 196, 244
Hysterical (hysteria, hysteric), 28, 116, 119, 157, 238, 239, 241

Id, 117, 118, 143, 147, 202, 230, 242
Identification, 129, 170, 205, 215, 216, 238, 240, 242

Index of Subjects

Identity, 98, 156, 211, 240
Impotence, 27–29, 32, 186
Individual dynamics, 55
Individual ego, 59, 64
Individualism (individualistic), 63, 65, 67, 68
Infantile, 13, 15, 16, 17, 27, 29, 30, 31, 33, 115, 117, 126–129, 161, 172, 173, 230, 235, 240
Infantile libidinal impulses, 120
Infantile neurosis, 117
Infantile sexuality, 118, 119, 242
Inferiority (inferior), 21, 24, 32, 115, 116, 120
Insight, 34, 85, 89, 110–112, 115, 123–125, 127, 202, 203, 223, 229
Insight-oriented psychotherapy, 81–83, 85, 90
Instinct (instinctual), 19, 45, 235
Interpersonal, 92, 93, 97, 98, 100, 119, 223
Interpretation (interpret), 22, 31, 38, 40, 41, 47, 51, 58, 61, 67, 68, 89, 111, 124, 127, 129, 130, 131, 139–141, 178, 184, 219, 220, 223, 229, 241, 242

Lesbian, 243, 244
Libido, 238
Libido theory, 119
Lobotomy, 146

Mania, 23, 24
Manic depressive, vii, 238, 239, 241–243, 248
Masochistic, 28, 110, 116
Masturbation, 228, 229, 237, 238
Maturational, 173
(Emotional) maturation, 57, 98, 114, 129
Maturity (mature), 31, 161, 170, 171, 238
Megalomania, 24
Multiple personalities, 216–217

Narcissistic, 49, 144, 168, 173, 184, 239
Narcissistic neuroses, 39
Narcissistic tendencies, 39
Narcoanalysis, 150
Narcotherapy, 150
Needs, 38, 41, 42, 49, 99, 101, 148, 178, 180, 186, 187, 213, 235
Negativism, 21

Neurasthenia (neurasthenic), 27, 239
Neurosis (neurotic), 6, 12, 14, 17, 18, 21, 24–34, 45, 63, 79, 84–86, 95, 97, 98, 111, 116–118, 122, 125, 128, 162, 167, 170–172, 202, 209–213, 218, 223, 237, 239, 245, 249
Neurosurgery, 151
Neurotic symptoms, 38, 39, 92, 123, 218

Object cathexes, 238
Object-choice, 15
Object-hypercathected, 238
Object needs, 42
Object relationship, 41, 42, 48
Obsessional (obsessive), 217, 238, 239
Obsessional neurosis, 142, 146
Oedipus (Oedipal), 146, 170, 228–230, 235, 241
Ontogenesis, 161
Organization man, 62, 63, 65

Paranoid (paranoic), 142, 154, 158, 242, 243, 246
Paranoid schizophrenic psychosis, 212, 232, 246
Pathodynamics, 107, 121, 126
Pathogenic, 33
Pathogenic defense, 51
Pharmacological treatment, 151
Phobia (phobic), 75, 116, 196, 217, 239
Phylogenesis, 160, 161
Pleasure-principle, 19, 238
Praxiological propositions, 77
Preconscious, 133, 203, 214, 215, 219, 220
Protestant Ethic, 61
Pseudomasochism, 28
Psychodynamic, 57, 58, 65, 68, 69, 121, 214, 215
Psychoneurosis (psychoneurotic), 20, 135, 136, 139, 142, 212
Psychoneurotic depression, 212
Psychopath (psychopathic), 238, 239, 242, 244
Psychopathologic processes, 53, 209
Psychosexual, 116, 142, 238
Psychosocial, 239
Psychosis (psychotic), 21, 39, 45, 136, 142, 144, 174, 197, 198, 218, 239, 248
Psychosomatic (symptoms), 122, 154, 158, 159, 248, 249

259

Psychotherapeutic, 59, 62, 68, 75, 101, 153, 155–157, 165, 178, 204, 209, 216, 222, 233, 243
Psychotherapeutic procedures, vii, 58, 205, 215
Psychotherapeutic process, vii, viii, 217, 221

Reaction formation, 160, 166, 243
Reality (real), 25, 30, 75, 79, 93, 99, 101, 121, 126, 146, 157, 166, 171, 230, 234, 241, 245
Reality testing, 39
Real self, 192
Recidivists, 27
Reconditioning, 113
Regression (regressive), 39, 40, 178, 192, 236
Regressive dependence, 41
Rejection (rejected), 127, 238, 240–242, 244
Repetition-compulsion, 231
Repression, 3, 9, 10, 11, 13, 185, 230
Research, vii, 71, 73, 74, 76–78, 80, 91, 101, 170, 208, 209, 221, 248
Resistance, 7, 8, 14, 16, 18, 21–34, 38, 44–47, 51, 123, 143, 144, 160, 162, 163, 165, 167, 170, 171, 176, 183, 185, 189, 222, 229, 230, 241, 244

Sadistic (sadism), 50, 116, 238
Sado-masochistic, 49, 239
Schizoid, 144, 238
Schizoid personality, 48, 154
Schizophrenia (schizophrenic), vii, 141, 154, 156, 195, 199, 236, 237–240, 243, 246–248
Self-cathexes, 238
Self-concept, 87, 93
Self-esteem, 92, 97, 241
Self-hypercathected, 238
Self-image, 114, 129
Self-realization, 87
Separation, 189, 191
Separation anxiety, 190, 228
Sexual (sexually), 8, 13, 19, 25–27, 31–33, 115, 116, 118, 120, 122, 136, 171, 182, 186, 226, 228–230, 237, 238, 243, 244
Social, 21, 31, 34, 62, 66, 69, 97, 99, 136, 146, 179, 194, 209, 211, 227, 237, 246

Social needs, 74
Socioeconomic, 53, 54, 57, 60, 61–63, 68, 69
Sociologic (sociological), 54, 64, 234, 251
Sociopathic, 239
Sociophilosophic, 53, 54
Sociopolitical, 53, 54, 57, 62, 68, 69
Sociotherapy, 150
Somatic, 153, 156, 157, 159
Somato-psychic interaction, 153–159
Suicide, 153, 187, 188, 197, 201, 246
Superego, 51, 110, 111, 113, 117–122, 128, 129, 143, 176, 215, 229, 230, 242, 246
Supportive psychotherapy, 38, 39, 154, 158
Symptom-formation, 135
Symptoms (symptomatic), 21, 44, 75, 76, 79, 85–87, 90, 92, 93, 97, 118, 119, 122, 142, 143, 146, 147, 156, 157, 181–183, 195, 196, 210, 211, 214, 223, 238, 245, 249
Syphilophobia, 32
Systematic desensitization, 81–83, 90, 112

Technologic, 54
Transference, viii, ix, 3–20 (love), 23, 33, 38–41, 43, 45–47, 59, 108, 111, 115, 120–123, 128, 134, 139, 143, 161, 163, 166–168, 171, 173, 185, 192, 194, 203, 219, 234–237, 240–242, 245–247
Transference neuroses, 38, 39, 170
Transference resistances, 46, 143, 229–230
Trauma (traumatic), 30, 95, 107, 112, 120, 149

Unconscious, viii, 13, 19, 30, 40, 59, 63, 116, 124, 133, 145, 147, 162, 167, 179, 194, 202, 203, 214, 215, 219, 220, 225, 230, 241, 248, 250
Unconscious conflicts, 38–40, 67

Vectoriasis praecox, 239
Voyeuristic, 50

Withdrawal (withdrawn), 21, 155, 184, 227, 236, 247